ΑΡΙΣΤΟΦΑΝΟΥΣ ARISTOPHANES'
Λυσιστράτη *Lysistrata*

A Dual Language Edition

Greek Text Edited by
F. W. Hall and W. M. Geldart

English Translation and Notes by
Ian Johnston

Edited by
Evan Hayes and Stephen Nimis

FAENUM PUBLISHING
OXFORD, OHIO

Aristophanes' Lysistrata: *A Dual Language Edition*
First Edition

© 2017 by Faenum Publishing

ISBN-10: 1940997976
ISBN-13: 9781940997971

Published by Faenum Publishing, Ltd.
Cover Design: Evan Hayes

for Geoffrey (1974-1997)

οἵη περ φύλλων γενεὴ τοίη δὲ καὶ ἀνδρῶν.
φύλλα τὰ μέν τ' ἄνεμος χαμάδις χέει, ἄλλα δέ θ' ὕλη
τηλεθόωσα φύει, ἔαρος δ' ἐπιγίγνεται ὥρη:
ὣς ἀνδρῶν γενεὴ ἣ μὲν φύει ἣ δ' ἀπολήγει.

Generations of men are like the leaves.
In winter, winds blow them down to earth,
but then, when spring season comes again,
the budding wood grows more. And so with men:
one generation grows, another dies away.   (*Iliad* 6)

TABLE OF CONTENTS

EDITORS' NOTE

This book presents the Greek text of Aristophanes' *Lysistrata* with a facing English translation. The Greek text is that of F. W. Hall and W. M. Geldart (1907), from the Oxford Classical Texts series, which is in the public domain and available as a pdf. This text has also been digitized by the Perseus Project (perseus.tufts.edu). The English translation and accompanying notes are those of Ian Johnston of Vancouver Island University, Nanaimo, BC. This translation is available freely online (records.viu.ca/--johnstoi/). We have reset both texts, making a number of very minor corrections, and placed them on opposing pages. This facing-page format will be useful to those wishing to read the English translation while looking at the Greek version, or vice versa.

Note that some discrepancies exists between the Greek text and English translation. Occasionally readings from other editions of or commentaries on Aristophanes' Greek text are used, accounting for some minor departures from Hall and Geldart's edition.

HISTORICAL NOTE

Aristophanes (c. 446 BC to c. 386 BC) was the foremost writer of Old Comedy in classical Athens. His play *Lysistrata* was first performed in Athens in 411 BC, two years after the disastrous Sicilian Expedition, where Athens suffered an enormous defeat in the continuing war with Sparta and its allies (a conflict with lasted from 431 BC to 404 BC).

ΛΥΣΙΣΤΡΑΤΗ

LYSISTRATA

ΤΑ ΤΟΥ ΔΡΑΜΑΤΟΣ ΠΡΟΣΩΠΑ*

ΛΥΣΙΣΤΡΑΤΗ

ΚΑΛΟΝΙΚΗ

ΜΥΡΡΙΝΗ

ΛΑΜΠΙΤΩ

ΓΥΝΑΙΚΕΣ

ΠΡΟΒΟΥΛΟΣ

ΚΙΝΗΣΙΑΣ

ΠΑΙΣ ΚΙΝΗΣΙΟΥ

ΚΗΡΥΞ ΛΑΚΕΔΑΙΜΟΝΙΩΝ

ΧΟΡΟΣ ΓΕΡΟΝΤΩΝ

ΧΟΡΟΣ ΓΥΝΑΙΚΩΝ

ΠΡΕΣΒΕΙΣ ΛΑΚΕΔΑΙΜΟΝΙΩΝ

ΑΘΗΝΑΙΟΙ ΤΙΝΕΣ

* In his translation, Johnston further divides the roles into more specific ones, such as WOMAN A, WOMAN B, CHORUS LEADER, etc., and includes directions for non-speaking parts. Further discussion of roles and line attributions may be found in the notes.

DRAMATIS PERSONAE

LYSISTRATA: a young Athenian wife

CALONICE: a mature married woman

MYRRHINE: a very attractive teenage wife

LAMPITO: a strong young country wife from Sparta

ISMENIA: a women from Thebes

SCYTHIAN GIRL: one of Lysistrata's slaves

MAGISTRATE: an elderly Athenian with white hair

CINESIAS: husband of Myrrhine

CHILD: infant son of Myrrhine and Cinesias

MANES: servant nurse of the Child

HERALD: A Spartan envoy

CHORUS OF OLD MEN

CHORUS OF OLD WOMEN

ATHENIAN AMBASSADOR

SPARTAN AMBASSADOR

WOMAN A: one of the wives following Lysistrata

WOMAN B: one of the wives following Lysistrata

WOMAN C: one of the wives following Lysistrata

ARMED GUARDS: four police officials attending on the Magistrate

WOMEN: followers of Lysistrata

RECONCILIATION: a goddess of harmony

ATHENIAN DELEGATES

SPARTAN DELEGATES

SLAVES AND ATTENDANTS

Λυσιστράτη

ΛΥΣΙΣΤΡΑΤΗ
  ἀλλ' εἴ τις ἐς Βακχεῖον αὐτὰς ἐκάλεσεν,
  ἢ 's Πανὸς ἢ 'πὶ Κωλιάδ' ἢ 's Γενετυλλίδος,
  οὐδ' ἂν διελθεῖν ἦν ἂν ὑπὸ τῶν τυμπάνων.
  νῦν δ' οὐδεμία πάρεστιν ἐνταυθοῖ γυνή·
  πλὴν ἥ γ' ἐμὴ κωμῆτις ἥδ' ἐξέρχεται.   5
  χαῖρ' ὦ Καλονίκη.

ΚΑΛΟΝΙΚΗ
                    καὶ σύ γ' ὦ Λυσιστράτη.
  τί συντετάραξαι; μὴ σκυθρώπαζ' ὦ τέκνον.
  οὐ γὰρ πρέπει σοι τοξοποιεῖν τὰς ὀφρῦς.

ΛΥΣΙΣΤΡΑΤΗ
  ἀλλ' ὦ Καλονίκη κάομαι τὴν καρδίαν,
  καὶ πόλλ' ὑπὲρ ἡμῶν τῶν γυναικῶν ἄχθομαι,   10
  ὁτιὴ παρὰ μὲν τοῖς ἀνδράσιν νενομίσμεθα
  εἶναι πανοῦργοι—

ΚΑΛΟΝΙΚΗ
                  καὶ γάρ ἐσμεν νὴ Δία.

ΛΥΣΙΣΤΡΑΤΗ
  εἰρημένον δ' αὐταῖς ἀπαντᾶν ἐνθάδε
  βουλευσομέναισιν οὐ περὶ φαύλου πράγματος,
  εὕδουσι κοὐχ ἥκουσιν.   15

ΚΑΛΟΝΙΚΗ
                      ἀλλ' ὦ φιλτάτη
  ἥξουσι· χαλεπή τοι γυναικῶν ἔξοδος.
  ἡ μὲν γὰρ ἡμῶν περὶ τὸν ἄνδρ' ἐκύπτασεν,
  ἡ δ' οἰκέτην ἤγειρεν, ἡ δὲ παιδίον
  κατέκλινεν, ἡ δ' ἔλουσεν, ἡ δ' ἐψώμισεν.

4

Lysistrata

[The action of the play takes place in a street in Athens, with the citadel on the Acropolis in the back, its doors facing the audience]

LYSISTRATA

> If they'd called a Bacchic celebration
> or some festival for Pan or Colias
> or for Genetyllis, you'd not be able
> to move around through all the kettle drums.
> But as it is, there are no women here.

[Calonice enters, coming to meet Lysistrata]

> Ah, here's my neighbour—at least she's come.[1]
> Hello, Calonice.

CALONICE

>   Hello, Lysistrata.
> What's bothering you, child? Don't look so annoyed.
> It doesn't suit you. Your eyes get wrinkled.

LYSISTRATA

> My heart's on fire, Calonice—I'm so angry   [10]
> at married women, at us, because,
> although men say we're devious characters . . .

CALONICE *[interrupting]*

> Because, by god, we are!

LYSISTRATA *[continuing]*

>   . . . when I call them all
> to meet here to discuss some serious business,
> they just stay in bed and don't show up.

CALONICE

> Ah, my dear, they'll come. It's not so easy
> for wives to get away. We've got to fuss
> about our husbands, wake up the servants,
> calm and wash the babies, then give them food.

5

ΛΥΣΙΣΤΡΑΤΗ

    ἀλλ᾽ ἕτερά τἄρ᾽ ἦν τῶνδε προὐργιαίτερα   20
    αὐταῖς.

ΚΑΛΟΝΙΚΗ

        τί δ᾽ ἐστὶν ὦ φίλη Λυσιστράτη,
    ἐφ᾽ ὅ τι ποθ᾽ ἡμᾶς τὰς γυναῖκας συγκαλεῖς;
    τί τὸ πρᾶγμα; πηλίκον τι;

ΛΥΣΙΣΤΡΑΤΗ

               μέγα.

ΚΑΛΟΝΙΚΗ

                  μῶν καὶ παχύ;

ΛΥΣΙΣΤΡΑΤΗ

    καὶ νὴ Δία παχύ.

ΚΑΛΟΝΙΚΗ

        κᾆτα πῶς οὐχ ἥκομεν;

ΛΥΣΙΣΤΡΑΤΗ

    οὐχ οὗτος ὁ τρόπος· ταχὺ γὰρ ἂν ξυνήλθομεν.   25
    ἀλλ᾽ ἔστιν ὑπ᾽ ἐμοῦ πρᾶγμ᾽ ἀνεζητημένον
    πολλαῖσί τ᾽ ἀγρυπνίαισιν ἐριπτασμένον.

ΚΑΛΟΝΙΚΗ

    ἦ πού τι λεπτόν ἐστι τοὐριπτασμένον.

ΛΥΣΙΣΤΡΑΤΗ

    οὕτω γε λεπτὸν ὥσθ᾽ ὅλης τῆς Ἑλλάδος
    ἐν ταῖς γυναιξίν ἐστιν ἡ σωτηρία.   30

ΚΑΛΟΝΙΚΗ

    ἐν ταῖς γυναιξίν; ἐπ᾽ ὀλίγου γ᾽ ὠχεῖτ᾽ ἄρα.

ΛΥΣΙΣΤΡΑΤΗ

    ὡς ἔστ᾽ ἐν ἡμῖν τῆς πόλεως τὰ πράγματα,
    ἢ μηκέτ᾽ εἶναι μήτε Πελοποννησίους

LYSISTRATA
But there are other things they need to do—   [20]
more important issues.

CALONICE
My dear Lysistrata,
why have you asked the women to meet here?
What's going on? Is it something big?

LYSISTRATA
It's huge.

CALONICE
And hard as well?

LYSISTRATA
Yes, by god, really hard.

CALONICE
Then why aren't we all here?

LYSISTRATA
I don't mean that!
If that were it, they'd all be charging here so fast.
No. It's something I've been playing with—
wrestling with for many sleepless nights.

CALONICE
If you've been working it like that, by now
it must have shrivelled up.

LYSISTRATA
Yes, so shrivelled up
that the salvation of the whole of Greece   [30]
is now in women's hands.

CALONICE
In women's hands?
Then it won't be long before we done for.

LYSISTRATA
It's up to us to run the state's affairs—
the Spartans would no longer be around.

ΚΑΛΟΝΙΚΗ

βέλτιστα τοίνυν μηκέτ᾽ εἶναι νὴ Δία.

ΛΥΣΙΣΤΡΑΤΗ

Βοιωτίους τε πάντας ἐξολωλέναι.   35

ΚΑΛΟΝΙΚΗ

μὴ δῆτα πάντας γ᾽, ἀλλ᾽ ἄφελε τὰς ἐγχέλεις.

ΛΥΣΙΣΤΡΑΤΗ

περὶ τῶν Ἀθηνῶν δ᾽ οὐκ ἐπιγλωττήσομαι
τοιοῦτον οὐδέν· ἀλλ᾽ ὑπονόησον σύ μοι.
ἢν δὲ ξυνέλθωσ᾽ αἱ γυναῖκες ἐνθάδε
αἵ τ᾽ ἐκ Βοιωτῶν αἵ τε Πελοποννησίων   40
ἡμεῖς τε, κοινῇ σώσομεν τὴν Ἑλλάδα.

ΚΑΛΟΝΙΚΗ

τί δ᾽ ἂν γυναῖκες φρόνιμον ἐργασαίατο
ἢ λαμπρόν, αἳ καθήμεθ᾽ ἐξηνθισμέναι,
κροκωτοφοροῦσαι καὶ κεκαλλωπισμέναι
καὶ Κιμμερίκ᾽ ὀρθοστάδια καὶ περιβαρίδας;   45

ΛΥΣΙΣΤΡΑΤΗ

ταῦτ᾽ αὐτὰ γάρ τοι κᾆσθ᾽ ἃ σώσειν προσδοκῶ,
τὰ κροκωτίδια καὶ τὰ μύρα χαἰ περιβαρίδες
χἤγχουσα καὶ τὰ διαφανῆ χιτώνια.

ΚΑΛΟΝΙΚΗ

τίνα δὴ τρόπον ποθ᾽;

ΛΥΣΙΣΤΡΑΤΗ

                        ὥστε τῶν νῦν μηδένα
ἀνδρῶν ἐπ᾽ ἀλλήλοισιν ἄρεσθαι δόρυ—   50

ΚΑΛΟΝΙΚΗ

κροκωτὸν ἄρα νὴ τὼ θεὼ ᾽γὼ βάψομαι.

8

CALONICE

    If they weren't there, by god, not any more,
    that would be good news.

LYSISTRATA

                    And then if all Boeotians
    were totally destroyed!

CALONICE

                         Not all of them—
    you'd have to save the eels.[2]

LYSISTRATA

                   As for Athens,
    I won't say anything as bad as that.
    You can imagine what I'd say. But now,
    if only all the women would come here
    from Sparta and Boeotia, join up with us,   [40]
    if we worked together, we'd save Greece.

CALONICE

    But what sensible or splendid act
    could women do? We sit around playing
    with our cosmetics, wearing golden clothes,
    posing in Cimmerian silks and slippers.

LYSISTRATA

    Those are the very things which I assume
    will save us—short dresses, perfumes, slippers,
    make up, and clothing men can see through.

CALONICE

    How's that going to work?

LYSISTRATA

                    No man living
    will lift his spear against another man . . .   [50]

CALONICE *[interrupting]*

    By the two goddesses, I must take my dress
    and dye it yellow.[3]

ΛΥΣΙΣΤΡΑΤΗ
  μηδ' ἀσπίδα λαβεῖν—

ΚΑΛΟΝΙΚΗ
              Κιμμερικὸν ἐνδύσομαι.

ΛΥΣΙΣΤΡΑΤΗ
  μηδὲ ξιφίδιον.

ΚΑΛΟΝΙΚΗ
          κτήσομαι περιβαρίδας.

ΛΥΣΙΣΤΡΑΤΗ
  ἆρ' οὐ παρεῖναι τὰς γυναῖκας δῆτ' ἐχρῆν;

ΚΑΛΟΝΙΚΗ
  οὐ γὰρ μὰ Δί' ἀλλὰ πετομένας ἥκειν πάλαι.   55

ΛΥΣΙΣΤΡΑΤΗ
  ἀλλ' ὦ μέλ' ὄψει τοι σφόδρ' αὐτὰς Ἀττικάς,
  ἅπαντα δρώσας τοῦ δέοντος ὕστερον.
  ἀλλ' οὐδὲ Παράλων οὐδεμία γυνὴ πάρα,
  οὐδ' ἐκ Σαλαμῖνος.

ΚΑΛΟΝΙΚΗ
                  ἀλλ' ἐκεῖναί γ' οἶδ' ὅτι
  ἐπὶ τῶν κελήτων διαβεβήκασ' ὄρθριαι.   60

ΛΥΣΙΣΤΡΑΤΗ
  οὐδ' ἃς προσεδόκων κἀλογιζόμην ἐγὼ
  πρώτας παρέσεσθαι δεῦρο τὰς Ἀχαρνέων
  γυναῖκας, οὐχ ἥκουσιν.

ΚΑΛΟΝΙΚΗ
                      ἡ γοῦν Θεογένους
  ὡς δεῦρ' ἰοῦσα θοὐκάταιον ἤρετο.
  ἀτὰρ αἵδε καὶ δή σοι προσέρχονταί τινες.   65
  αἱδί θ' ἕτεραι χωροῦσί τινες. ἰοὺ ἰού,
  πόθεν εἰσίν;

LYSISTRATA *[continuing]*
> . . . or pick up a shield . . .

CALONICE *[interrupting again]*
> I'll have to wear my very best silk dress.

LYSISTRATA *[continuing]*
> . . . or pull out his sword.

CALONICE
> I need to get some shoes.

LYSISTRATA
> O these women, they should be here by now!

CALONICE
> Yes, by god! They should have sprouted wings
> and come here hours ago.

LYSISTRATA
> They're true Athenians,
> you'll see—everything they should be doing
> they postpone till later. But no one's come
> from Salamis or those towns on the coast.

CALONICE *[with an obscene gesture]*
> I know those women—they were up early
> on their boats riding the mizzen mast.

[60]

LYSISTRATA
> I'd have bet
> those women from Acharnia would come
> and get here first. But they've not shown up.

CALONICE
> Well, Theogenes' wife will be here.
> I saw her hoisting sail to come.[4] Hey, look!
> Here's a group of women coming for you.
> And there's another one, as well. Hello!
> Hello there! Where they from?

[Various women start arriving from all directions]

ΛΥΣΙΣΤΡΑΤΗ
  Ἀναγυρουντόθεν.

ΚΑΛΟΝΙΚΗ
     νὴ τὸν Δία·
ὁ γοῦν ἀνάγυρός μοι κεκινῆσθαι δοκεῖ.

ΜΥΡΡΙΝΗ
  μῶν ὕστεραι πάρεσμεν ὦ Λυσιστράτη;
  τί φῄς; τί σιγᾷς;

ΛΥΣΙΣΤΡΑΤΗ
     οὔ σ᾽ ἐπαινῶ Μυρίνη   70
ἤκουσαν ἄρτι περὶ τοιούτου πράγματος.

ΜΥΡΡΙΝΗ
  μόλις γὰρ ηὗρον ἐν σκότῳ τὸ ζώνιον.
  ἀλλ᾽ εἴ τι πάνυ δεῖ, ταῖς παρούσαισιν λέγε.

ΛΥΣΙΣΤΡΑΤΗ
  μὰ Δί᾽ ἀλλ᾽ ἐπαναμείνωμεν ὀλίγου γ᾽ οὕνεκα
  τάς τ᾽ ἐκ Βοιωτῶν τάς τε Πελοποννησίων   75
  γυναῖκας ἐλθεῖν.

ΜΥΡΡΙΝΗ
     πολὺ σὺ κάλλιον λέγεις.
ἡδὶ δὲ καὶ δὴ Λαμπιτὼ προσέρχεται.

ΛΥΣΙΣΤΡΑΤΗ
  ὦ φιλτάτη Λάκαινα χαῖρε Λαμπιτοῖ.
  οἷον τὸ κάλλος γλυκυτάτη σου φαίνεται.
  ὡς δ᾽ εὐχροεῖς, ὡς δὲ σφριγᾷ τὸ σῶμά σου.   80
  κἂν ταῦρον ἄγχοις.

ΛΑΜΠΙΤΩ
     μάλα γ᾽ οἰῶ ναὶ τὼ σιώ·
γυμνάδδομαι γὰρ καὶ ποτὶ πυγὰν ἅλλομαι.

LYSISTRATA

          Those? From Anagyrus.

CALONICE

    My god, it seems we're kicking up a stink.[5]

[Enter Myrrhine]

MYRRHINE

    Hey, Lysistrata, did we get here late?
    What's the matter? Why are you so quiet?

LYSISTRATA

    I'm not pleased with you, Myrrhine. You're late.   [70]
    And this is serious business.

MYRRHINE

                It was dark.
    I had trouble tracking down my waist band.
    If it's such a big deal, tell these women.

LYSISTRATA

    No, let's wait a while until the women
    from Sparta and Boeotia get here.

MYRRHINE

    All right. That sounds like the best idea.
    Hey, here comes Lampito.

[Lampito enters with some other Spartan women and with Ismenia, a woman from Thebes]

LYSISTRATA

              Hello Lampito,
    my dear friend from Sparta. How beautiful
    you look, so sweet, such a fine complexion.   [80]
    And your body looks so fit, strong enough
    to choke a bull.

LAMPITO[6]

            Yes, by the two gods,
    I could pull that off.[7] I do exercise
    and work out to keep my butt well toned.

13

ΚΑΛΟΝΙΚΗ
 ὡς δὴ καλὸν τὸ χρῆμα τιτθίων ἔχεις.

ΛΑΜΠΙΤΩ
 ᾇπερ ἱερεῖόν τοί μ' ὑποψαλάσσετε.

ΛΥΣΙΣΤΡΑΤΗ
 ἠδὶ δὲ ποδαπή 'σθ' ἡ νεᾶνις ἡτέρα;   85

ΛΑΜΠΙΤΩ
 πρέσβειρά τοι ναὶ τὼ σιὼ Βοιωτία
 ἵκει ποθ' ὑμέ.

ΜΥΡΡΙΝΗ
    νὴ μὰ Δία Βοιωτία,
 καλόν γ' ἔχουσα τὸ πεδίον.

ΚΑΛΟΝΙΚΗ
      καὶ νὴ Δία
 κομψότατα τὴν βληχώ γε παρατετιλμένη.

ΛΥΣΙΣΤΡΑΤΗ
 τίς δ' ἡτέρα παῖς;   90

ΛΑΜΠΙΤΩ
    χαΐα ναὶ τὼ σιώ,
 Κορινθία δ' αὖ.

ΚΑΛΟΝΙΚΗ
    χαΐα νὴ τὸν Δία
 δήλη 'στὶν οὖσα ταυταγὶ τἀντευθενί.

ΛΑΜΠΙΤΩ
 τίς δ' αὖ ξυναλίαξε τόνδε τὸν στόλον
 τὸν τᾶν γυναικῶν;

ΛΥΣΙΣΤΡΑΤΗ
    ἥδ' ἐγώ.

ΛΑΜΠΙΤΩ
     μύσιδδέ τοι
 ὅ τι λῇς ποθ' ἁμέ.   95

14

CALONICE *[fondling Lampito's bosom]*
> What an amazing pair of breasts you've got!

LAMPITO
> O, you stroke me like I'm a sacrifice.

LYSISTRATA *[looking at Ismenia]*
> And this young woman—where's she from?   [90]

LAMPITO
> By the twin gods, she's an ambassador—
> she's from Boeotia.

MYRRHINE *[looking down Ismenia's elegant clothes]*
>   Of course, from Boeotia.
> She's got a beautiful lowland region.

CALONICE *[peering down Ismenia's dress to see her pubic hair]*
> Yes. By god, she keeps that territory
> elegantly groomed.

LYSISTRATA
>   Who's the other girl?

LAMPITO
> A noble girl, by the two gods, from Corinth.

CALONICE *[inspecting the girl's bosom and buttocks]*
> A really noble girl, by Zeus—it's clear
> she's got good lines right here, back here as well.

LAMPITO
> All right, who's the one who called the meeting
> and brought this bunch of women here?

LYSISTRATA
>   I did.

LAMPITO
> Then lay out what it is you want from us.

15

Aristophanes

ΜΥΡΡΙΝΗ

νὴ Δί᾿ ὦ φίλη γύναι,
λέγε δῆτα τὸ σπουδαῖον ὅ τι τοῦτ᾿ ἐστί σοι.

ΛΥΣΙΣΤΡΑΤΗ

λέγοιμ᾿ ἂν ἤδη. πρὶν λέγειν ⟨δ᾿⟩, ὑμᾶς τοδὶ
ἐπερήσομαί τι μικρόν.

ΚΑΛΟΝΙΚΗ

ὅ τι βούλει γε σύ.

ΛΥΣΙΣΤΡΑΤΗ

τοὺς πατέρας οὐ ποθεῖτε τοὺς τῶν παιδίων
ἐπὶ στρατιᾶς ἀπόντας; εὖ γὰρ οἶδ᾿ ὅτι   100
πάσαισιν ὑμῖν ἐστιν ἀποδημῶν ἀνήρ.

ΚΑΛΟΝΙΚΗ

ὁ γοῦν ἐμὸς ἀνὴρ πέντε μῆνας ὦ τάλαν
ἄπεστιν ἐπὶ Θρᾴκης φυλάττων Εὐκράτη.

ΜΥΡΡΙΝΗ

ὁ δ᾿ ἐμός γε τελέους ἑπτὰ μῆνας ἐν Πύλῳ.

ΛΑΜΠΙΤΩ

ὁ δ᾿ ἐμός γα καὶ κ᾿ ἐκ τᾶς ταγᾶς ἔλσῃ ποκά,   105
πορπακισάμενος φροῦδος ἀμπτάμενος ἔβα.

ΛΥΣΙΣΤΡΑΤΗ

ἀλλ᾿ οὐδὲ μοιχοῦ καταλέλειπται φεψάλυξ.
ἐξ οὗ γὰρ ἡμᾶς προὔδοσαν Μιλήσιοι,
οὐκ εἶδον οὐδ᾿ ὄλισβον ὀκτωδάκτυλον,
ὃς ἦν ἂν ἡμῖν σκυτίνη ᾿πικουρία.   110
ἐθέλοιτ᾿ ἂν οὖν, εἰ μηχανὴν εὕροιμ᾿ ἐγώ,
μετ᾿ ἐμοῦ καταλῦσαι τὸν πόλεμον;

ΜΥΡΡΙΝΗ

νὴ τὼ θεώ·
ἔγωγ᾿ ἂν ⟨οὖν⟩ κἂν εἴ με χρείη τοὔγκυκλον
τουτὶ καταθεῖσαν ἐκπιεῖν αὐθημερόν.

16

MYRRHINE

Come on, dear lady, tell us what's going on,
what's so important to you.

LYSISTRATA

In a minute.
Before I say it, I'm going to ask you
one small question.

CALONICE

Ask whatever you want.

LYSISTRATA

Don't you miss the fathers of your children
when they go off to war? I understand   [100]
you all have husbands far away from home.

CALONICE

My dear, it's five full months my man's been gone—
off in Thrace taking care of Eucrates.

MYRRHINE

And mine's been stuck in Pylos seven whole months.[8]

LAMPITO

And mine—as soon as he gets home from war
he grabs his shield and buggers off again.

LYSISTRATA

As for old flames and lovers—they're none left.
And since Milesians went against us,
I've not seen a decent eight-inch dildo.
Yes, it's just leather, but it helps us out.[9]   [110]
So would you be willing, if I found a way,
to work with me to make this fighting end?

MYRRHINE

By the twin goddesses, yes. Even if
in just one day I had to pawn this dress
and drain my purse.

ΚΑΛΟΝΙΚΗ

 ἐγὼ δέ γ' ἂν κἂν ὡσπερεὶ ψῆτταν δοκῶ   115
 δοῦναι ἂν ἐμαυτῆς παρατεμοῦσα θἤμισυ.

ΛΑΜΠΙΤΩ

 ἐγὼ δὲ καί κα ποττὸ Ταΰγετόν γ' ἄνω
 ἔλσοιμ' ὅπα μέλλοιμί γ' εἰράναν ἰδεῖν.

ΛΥΣΙΣΤΡΑΤΗ

 λέγοιμ' ἄν· οὐ δεῖ γὰρ κεκρύφθαι τὸν λόγον.
 ἡμῖν γὰρ ὦ γυναῖκες, εἴπερ μέλλομεν   120
 ἀναγκάσειν τοὺς ἄνδρας εἰρήνην ἄγειν,
 ἀφεκτέ' ἐστὶ—

ΜΥΡΡΙΝΗ

     τοῦ; φράσον.

ΛΥΣΙΣΤΡΑΤΗ

       ποιήσετ' οὖν;

ΜΥΡΡΙΝΗ

 ποιήσομεν, κἂν ἀποθανεῖν ἡμᾶς δέῃ.

ΛΥΣΙΣΤΡΑΤΗ

 ἀφεκτέα τοίνυν ἐστὶν ἡμῖν τοῦ πέους.
 τί μοι μεταστρέφεσθε; ποῖ βαδίζετε;   125
 αὗται τί μοιμυᾶτε κἀνανεύετε;
 τί χρὼς τέτραπται; τί δάκρυον κατείβεται;
 ποιήσετ' ἢ οὐ ποιήσετ'; ἢ τί μέλλετε;

ΜΥΡΡΙΝΗ

 οὐκ ἂν ποιήσαιμ', ἀλλ' ὁ πόλεμος ἑρπέτω.

ΚΑΛΟΝΙΚΗ

 μὰ Δί' οὐδ' ἐγὼ γάρ, ἀλλ' ὁ πόλεμος ἑρπέτω.   130

CALONICE
                    Me too—they could slice me up
like a flat fish, then use one half of me
to get a peace.

LAMPITO
                    I'd climb up to the top
of Taygetus to get a glimpse of peace.[10]

LYSISTRATA
    All right I'll tell you. No need to keep quiet
    about my plan. Now, ladies, if we want   [120]
    to force the men to have a peace, well then,
    we must give up . . .

MYRRHINE *[interrupting]*
                    Give up what? Tell us!

LYSISTRATA
    Then, will you do it?

MYRRHINE
                    Of course, we'll do it,
    even if we have to die.

LYSISTRATA
                    All right then—
    we have to give up all male penises.

[The women react with general consternation]

    Why do you turn away? Where are you going?
    How come you bite your lips and shake your heads?
    And why so pale? How come you're crying like that?
    Will you do it or not? What will it be?

MYRRHINE
    I won't do it. So let the war drag on.

CALONICE
    I won't either. The war can keep on going.   [130]

19

ΛΥΣΙΣΤΡΑΤΗ

   ταυτὶ σὺ λέγεις ὦ ψῆττα; καὶ μὴν ἄρτι γε
   ἔφησθα σαυτῆς κἂν παρατεμεῖν θἤμισυ.

ΚΑΛΟΝΙΚΗ

   ἀλλ᾽ ἀλλ᾽ ὅ τι βούλει· κἂν με χρῇ διὰ τοῦ πυρὸς
   ἐθέλω βαδίζειν· τοῦτο μᾶλλον τοῦ πέους.
   οὐδὲν γὰρ οἷον ὦ φίλη Λυσιστράτη.   135

ΛΥΣΙΣΤΡΑΤΗ

   τί δαὶ σύ;

ΜΥΡΡΙΝΗ

        κἀγὼ βούλομαι διὰ τοῦ πυρός.

ΛΥΣΙΣΤΡΑΤΗ

   ὦ παγκατάπυγον θἠμέτερον ἅπαν γένος,
   οὐκ ἐτὸς ἀφ᾽ ἡμῶν εἰσιν αἱ τραγῳδίαι.
   οὐδὲν γάρ ἐσμεν πλὴν Ποσειδῶν καὶ σκάφη.
   ἀλλ᾽ ὦ φίλη Λάκαινα, σὺ γὰρ ἐὰν γένῃ   140
   μόνη μετ᾽ ἐμοῦ, τὸ πρᾶγμ᾽ ἀνασωσαίμεσθ᾽ ἔτ᾽ ⟨ἄν⟩,
   ξυμψήφισαί μοι.

ΛΑΜΠΙΤΩ

        χαλεπὰ μὲν ναὶ τὼ σιὼ
   γυναῖκάς ἐσθ᾽ ὕπνων ἄνευ ψωλᾶς μόνας.
   ὅμως γα μάν· δεῖ τᾶς γὰρ εἰράνας μάλ᾽ αὖ.

ΛΥΣΙΣΤΡΑΤΗ

   ὦ φιλτάτη σὺ καὶ μόνη τούτων γυνή.   145

ΚΑΛΟΝΙΚΗ

   εἰ δ᾽ ὡς μάλιστ᾽ ἀπεχοίμεθ᾽ οὗ σὺ δὴ λέγεις,
   ὃ μὴ γένοιτο, μᾶλλον ἂν διὰ τουτογὶ
   γένοιτ᾽ ἂν εἰρήνη;

ΛΥΣΙΣΤΡΑΤΗ

        πολύ γε νὴ τὼ θεώ.
   εἰ γὰρ καθοίμεθ᾽ ἔνδον ἐντετριμμέναι,

LYSISTRATA

How can you say that, you flatfish? Just now
you said they could slice you into halves.

CALONICE

Ask what you like, but not that! If I had to,
I'd be willing to walk through fire—sooner that
than give up screwing. There's nothing like it,
dear Lysistrata.

LYSISTRATA

And what about you?

MYRRHINE

I'd choose the fire, too.

LYSISTRATA

What a debased race
we women are! It's no wonder men write
tragedies about us. We're good for nothing
but screwing Poseidon in the bath tub.
But my Spartan friend, if you were willing,
just you and me, we still could pull it off.
So help me out.

[140]

LAMPITO

By the twin gods, it's hard
for women to sleep all by themselves
without a throbbing cock. But we must try.
We've got to have a peace.

LYSISTRATA

O you're a true friend!
The only real woman in this bunch.

CALONICE

If we really do give up what you say—
I hope it never happens!—would doing that
make peace more likely?

LYSISTRATA

By the two goddesses, yes,
much more likely. If we sit around at home

21

κἀν τοῖς χιτωνίοισι τοῖς Ἀμοργίνοις   150
γυμναὶ παρίοιμεν δέλτα παρατετιλμέναι,
στύοιντο δ᾽ ἄνδρες κἀπιθυμοῖεν σπλεκοῦν,
ἡμεῖς δὲ μὴ προσίοιμεν ἀλλ᾽ ἀπεχοίμεθα,
σπονδὰς ποιήσαιντ᾽ ἂν ταχέως, εὖ οἶδ᾽ ὅτι.

ΛΑΜΠΙΤΩ

ὁ γῶν Μενέλαος τᾶς Ἑλένας τὰ μᾶλά πα   155
γυμνᾶς παραϊδὼν ἐξέβαλ᾽, οἰῶ, τὸ ξίφος.

ΚΑΛΟΝΙΚΗ

τί δ᾽ ἢν ἀφιῶσ᾽ ἄνδρες ἡμᾶς ὦ μέλε;

ΛΥΣΙΣΤΡΑΤΗ

τὸ τοῦ Φερεκράτους, κύνα δέρειν δεδαρμένην.

ΚΑΛΟΝΙΚΗ

φλυαρία ταῦτ᾽ ἐστὶ τὰ μεμιμημένα.
ἐὰν λαβόντες δ᾽ ἐς τὸ δωμάτιον βίᾳ   160
ἕλκωσιν ἡμᾶς;

ΛΥΣΙΣΤΡΑΤΗ

          ἀντέχου σὺ τῶν θυρῶν.

ΚΑΛΟΝΙΚΗ

ἐὰν δὲ τύπτωσιν;

ΛΥΣΙΣΤΡΑΤΗ

          παρέχειν χρὴ κακὰ κακῶς.
οὐ γὰρ ἔνι τούτοις ἡδονὴ τοῖς πρὸς βίαν.
κἄλλως ὀδυνᾶν χρή· κἀμέλει ταχέως πάνυ
ἀπεροῦσιν. οὐ γὰρ οὐδέποτ᾽ εὐφρανθήσεται   165
ἀνήρ, ἐὰν μὴ τῇ γυναικὶ συμφέρῃ.

ΚΑΛΟΝΙΚΗ

εἴ τοι δοκεῖ σφῷν ταῦτα, χἠμῖν ξυνδοκεῖ.

with all our make up on and in those gowns
made of Amorgos silk, naked underneath, [150]
with our crotches neatly plucked, our husbands
will get hard and want to screw. But then,
if we stay away and won't come near them,
they'll make peace soon enough. I'm sure of it.

LAMPITO

Yes, just like they say—when Menelaus
saw Helen's naked tits, he dropped his sword.[11]

CALONICE

But my friend, what if our men ignore us?

LYSISTRATA

Well then, in the words of Pherecrates,
you'll find another way to skin the dog.[12]

CALONICE

But fake penises aren't any use at all.
What if they grab us and haul us by force [160]
into the bedroom.

LYSISTRATA

Just grab the door post.

CALONICE

And if they beat us?

LYSISTRATA

Then you must submit—
but do it grudgingly, don't cooperate.
There's no enjoyment for them when they just
force it in. Besides, there are other ways
to make them suffer. They'll soon surrender.
No husband ever had a happy life
if he did not get on well with his wife.

CALONICE

Well, if you two think it's good, we do, too.

23

ΛΑΜΠΙΤΩ

καὶ τὼς μὲν ἁμῶν ἄνδρας ἁμὲς πείσομες
παντᾷ δικαίως ἄδολον εἰράναν ἄγειν·
τὸν τῶν Ἀσαναίων γα μὰν ῥυάχετον   170
πᾷ κά τις ἀμπείσειεν αὖ μὴ πλαδδιῆν;

ΛΥΣΙΣΤΡΑΤΗ

ἡμεῖς ἀμέλει σοι τά γε παρ' ἡμῖν πείσομεν.

ΛΑΜΠΙΤΩ

οὐχ ᾆς πόδας κ' ἔχωντι ταὶ τριήρεες,
καὶ τὠργύριον τὤβυσσον ᾖ πὰρ τᾷ σιῷ.

ΛΥΣΙΣΤΡΑΤΗ

ἀλλ' ἔστι καὶ τοῦτ' εὖ παρεσκευασμένον·   175
καταληψόμεθα γὰρ τὴν ἀκρόπολιν τήμερον.
ταῖς πρεσβυτάταις γὰρ προστέτακται τοῦτο δρᾶν,
ἕως ἂν ἡμεῖς ταῦτα συντιθώμεθα,
θύειν δοκούσαις καταλαβεῖν τὴν ἀκρόπολιν.

ΛΑΜΠΙΤΩ

παντᾷ κ' ἔχοι, καὶ τᾷδε γὰρ λέγεις καλῶς.   180

ΛΥΣΙΣΤΡΑΤΗ

τί δῆτα ταῦτ' οὐχ ὡς τάχιστ' ὦ Λαμπιτοῖ
ξυνωμόσαμεν, ὅπως ἂν ἀρήκτως ἔχῃ;

ΛΑΜΠΙΤΩ

πάρφαινε μὰν τὸν ὅρκον, ὡς ὀμιόμεθα.

ΛΥΣΙΣΤΡΑΤΗ

καλῶς λέγεις. ποῦ 'σθ' ἡ Σκύθαινα; ποῖ βλέπεις;
θὲς ἐς τὸ πρόσθεν ὑπτίαν τὴν ἀσπίδα,   185
καί μοι δότω τὰ τόμιά τις.

LAMPITO
   I'm sure we can persuade our men to work
   for a just peace in everything, no tricks.
   But how'll you convince the Athenian mob?   [170]
   They're mad for war.

LYSISTRATA
                        That's not your worry.
   We'll win them over.

LAMPITO
                        I don't think so—
   not while they have triremes under sail
   and that huge treasure stashed away
   where your goddess makes her home.[13]

LYSISTRATA
   But that's all been well taken care of.
   Today we'll capture the Acropolis.
   The old women have been assigned the task.
   While we sit here planning all the details,
   they'll pretend they're going there to sacrifice
   and seize the place.

LAMPITO
                        You've got it all worked out.   [180]
   What you say sounds good.

LYSISTRATA
                        All right Lampito,
   let's swear an oath as quickly as we can.
   That way we'll be united.

LAMPITO
                        Recite the oath.
   Then we'll all swear to it.

LYSISTRATA
                        That's good advice.
      Where's that girl from Scythia?

[The Scythian slave steps forward. She's holding a small shield]

                        Why stare like that?
   Put down your shield, the hollow part on top.
   Now, someone get me a victim's innards.

ΚΑΛΟΝΙΚΗ

Λυσιστράτη
τίν᾽ ὅρκον ὁρκώσεις ποθ᾽ ἡμᾶς;

ΛΥΣΙΣΤΡΑΤΗ

ὅντινα;
εἰς ἀσπίδ᾽, ὥσπερ φάσ᾽ ἐν Αἰσχύλῳ ποτέ,
μηλοσφαγούσας.

ΚΑΛΟΝΙΚΗ

μὴ σύ γ᾽ ὦ Λυσιστράτη
εἰς ἀσπίδ᾽ ὀμόσῃς μηδὲν εἰρήνης πέρι.   190

ΛΥΣΙΣΤΡΑΤΗ

τίς ἂν οὖν γένοιτ᾽ ἂν ὅρκος;

ΚΑΛΟΝΙΚΗ

εἰ λευκόν ποθεν
ἵππον λαβοῦσαι τόμιον ἐντεμοίμεθα.

ΛΥΣΙΣΤΡΑΤΗ

ποῖ λευκὸν ἵππον;

ΚΑΛΟΝΙΚΗ

ἀλλὰ πῶς ὁμούμεθα
ἡμεῖς;

ΛΥΣΙΣΤΡΑΤΗ

ἐγώ σοι νὴ Δί᾽, ἢν βούλῃ, φράσω.
θεῖσαι μέλαιναν κύλικα μεγάλην ὑπτίαν,   195
μηλοσφαγοῦσαι Θάσιον οἴνου σταμνίον
ὀμόσωμεν ἐς τὴν κύλικα μὴ 'πιχεῖν ὕδωρ.

ΛΑΜΠΙΤΩ

φεῦ δᾶ τὸν ὅρκον ἄφατον ὡς ἐπαινίω.

ΛΥΣΙΣΤΡΑΤΗ

φερέτω κύλικά τις ἔνδοθεν καὶ σταμνίον.

ΚΑΛΟΝΙΚΗ

ὦ φίλταται γυναῖκες, <ὁ> κεραμεὼν ὅσος.   200
ταύτην μὲν ἄν τις εὐθὺς ἡσθείη λαβών.

CALONICE
>Lysistrata, what sort of oath is this
>we're going to swear?

LYSISTRATA
>What sort of oath?
>One on a shield, just like they did back then
>in Aeschylus' play—with slaughtered sheep.

CALONICE
>You can't, Lysistrata, not on a shield,
>you can't swear an oath for peace on that.   [190]

LYSISTRATA
>What should the oath be, then?

CALONICE
>Let's get a stallion,
>a white one, and then offer up its guts!

LYSISTRATA
>Why a white horse?

CALONICE
>Then how will we make our oath?

LYSISTRATA
>I'll tell you, by god, if you want to hear.
>Put a large dark bowl down on the ground,
>then sacrifice a jug of Thasian wine,
>and swear we'll never pour in water.

LAMPITO
>Now, if you ask me, that's a super oath!

LYSISTRATA
>Someone get the bowl and a jug of wine.

[The Scythian girl goes back in the house and returns with a bowl and a jug of wine. Calonice takes the bowl]

CALONICE
>Look, dear ladies, at this splendid bowl.   [200]
>Just touching this gives instant pleasure.

27

ΛΥΣΙΣΤΡΑΤΗ

καταθεῖσα ταύτην προσλαβοῦ μοι τοῦ κάπρου.
δέσποινα Πειθοῖ καὶ κύλιξ φιλοτησία,
τὰ σφάγια δέξαι ταῖς γυναιξὶν εὐμενής.

ΚΑΛΟΝΙΚΗ

εὔχρων γε θαῖμα κἀποπυτίζει καλῶς.   205

ΛΑΜΠΙΤΩ

καὶ μὰν ποτόδδει γ᾽ ἁδὺ ναὶ τὸν Κάστορα.

ΜΥΡΡΙΝΗ

ἐᾶτε πρώτην μ᾽ ὦ γυναῖκες ὀμνύναι.

ΚΑΛΟΝΙΚΗ

μὰ τὴν Ἀφροδίτην οὔκ, ἐάν γε μὴ λάχῃς.

ΛΥΣΙΣΤΡΑΤΗ

λάζυσθε πᾶσαι τῆς κύλικος ὦ Λαμπιτοῖ·
λεγέτω δ᾽ ὑπὲρ ὑμῶν μί᾽ ἅπερ ἂν κἀγὼ λέγω·   210
ὑμεῖς δ᾽ ἐπομεῖσθε ταὐτὰ κἀμπεδώσετε.
οὐκ ἔστιν οὐδεὶς οὔτε μοιχὸς οὔτ᾽ ἀνήρ—

ΚΑΛΟΝΙΚΗ

οὐκ ἔστιν οὐδεὶς οὔτε μοιχὸς οὔτ᾽ ἀνήρ—

ΛΥΣΙΣΤΡΑΤΗ

ὅστις πρὸς ἐμὲ πρόσεισιν ἐστυκώς. λέγε.

ΚΑΛΟΝΙΚΗ

ὅστις πρὸς ἐμὲ πρόσεισιν ἐστυκώς. παπαῖ   215
ὑπολύεταί μου τὰ γόνατ᾽ ὦ Λυσιστράτη.

ΛΥΣΙΣΤΡΑΤΗ

οἴκοι δ᾽ ἀταυρώτη διάξω τὸν βίον—

LYSISTRATA
>Put it down. Now join me and place your hands
>on our sacrificial victim.

[The women gather around the bowl and lay their hands on the wine jug. Lysistrata starts the ritual prayer]

>O you,
>Goddess of Persuasion and the bowl
>which we so love, accept this sacrifice,
>a women's offering, and be kind to us.

[Lysistrata opens the wine jug and lets the wine pour out into the bowl]

CALONICE
>Such healthy blood spurts out so beautifully!

LAMPITO
>By Castor, that's a mighty pleasant smell.

MYRRHINE
>Ladies, let me be the first to swear the oath.

CALONICE
>No, by Aphrodite, no—not unless
>your lot is drawn.

LYSISTRATA *[holds up a bowl full of wine]*
>Grab the brim, Lampito,
>you and all the others. Someone repeat
>for all the rest of you the words I say—
>that way you'll pledge your firm allegiance:
>No man, no husband and no lover . . .

[210]

CALONICE *[taking the oath]*
>No man, no husband and no lover . . .

LYSISTRATA
>. . . will get near me with a stiff prick. . . Come on . . .
>Say it!

CALONICE
>. . . will get near me with a stiff prick.
>O Lysistrata, my knees are getting weak!

LYSISTRATA
>At home I'll live completely without sex . . .

ΚΑΛΟΝΙΚΗ

    οἴκοι δ' ἀταυρώτη διάξω τὸν βίον—

ΛΥΣΙΣΤΡΑΤΗ

    κροκωτοφοροῦσα καὶ κεκαλλωπισμένη,—

ΚΑΛΟΝΙΚΗ

    κροκωτοφοροῦσα καὶ κεκαλλωπισμένη,—   220

ΛΥΣΙΣΤΡΑΤΗ

    ὅπως ἂν ἀνὴρ ἐπιτυφῇ μάλιστά μου·

ΚΑΛΟΝΙΚΗ

    ὅπως ἂν ἀνὴρ ἐπιτυφῇ μάλιστά μου·

ΛΥΣΙΣΤΡΑΤΗ

    κοὐδέποθ' ἑκοῦσα τἀνδρὶ τὠμῷ πείσομαι.

ΚΑΛΟΝΙΚΗ

    κοὐδέποθ' ἑκοῦσα τἀνδρὶ τὠμῷ πείσομαι.

ΛΥΣΙΣΤΡΑΤΗ

    ἐὰν δέ μ' ἄκουσαν βιάζηται βίᾳ,—   225

ΚΑΛΟΝΙΚΗ

    ἐὰν δέ μ' ἄκουσαν βιάζηται βίᾳ,—

ΛΥΣΙΣΤΡΑΤΗ

    κακῶς παρέξω κοὐχὶ προσκινήσομαι.

ΚΑΛΟΝΙΚΗ

    κακῶς παρέξω κοὐχὶ προσκινήσομαι.

ΛΥΣΙΣΤΡΑΤΗ

    οὐ πρὸς τὸν ὄροφον ἀνατενῶ τὼ Περσικά.

ΚΑΛΟΝΙΚΗ

    οὐ πρὸς τὸν ὄροφον ἀνατενῶ τὼ Περσικά.   230

ΛΥΣΙΣΤΡΑΤΗ

    οὐ στήσομαι λέαιν' ἐπὶ τυροκνήστιδος.

ΚΑΛΟΝΙΚΗ

    οὐ στήσομαι λέαιν' ἐπὶ τυροκνήστιδος.

CALONICE

　　At home I'll live completely without sex . . .

LYSISTRATA

　　. . . wearing saffron silks, with lots of make up . . .

CALONICE

　　. . . wearing saffron silks, with lots of make up . . .　　　　　[220]

LYSISTRATA

　　. . . to make my man as horny as I can.

CALONICE

　　. . . to make my man as horny as I can.

LYSISTRATA

　　If against my will he takes me by force . . .

CALONICE

　　If against my will he takes me by force . . .

LYSISTRATA

　　. . . I'll be a lousy lay, not move a limb.

CALONICE

　　. . . I'll be a lousy lay, not move a limb.

LYSISTRATA

　　I'll not raise my slippers up towards the roof . . .

CALONICE

　　I'll not raise my slippers up towards the roof . . .　　　　　[230]

LYSISTRATA

　　. . . nor crouch down like a lioness on all fours.

CALONICE

　　. . . nor crouch down like a lioness on all fours.

ΛΥΣΙΣΤΡΑΤΗ

ταῦτ᾽ ἐμπεδοῦσα μὲν πίοιμ᾽ ἐντευθενί·

ΚΑΛΟΝΙΚΗ

ταῦτ᾽ ἐμπεδοῦσα μὲν πίοιμ᾽ ἐντευθενί·

ΛΥΣΙΣΤΡΑΤΗ

εἰ δὲ παραβαίην, ὕδατος ἐμπλῇθ᾽ ἡ κύλιξ.   235

ΚΑΛΟΝΙΚΗ

εἰ δὲ παραβαίην, ὕδατος ἐμπλῇθ᾽ ἡ κύλιξ.

ΛΥΣΙΣΤΡΑΤΗ

συνεπόμνυθ᾽ ὑμεῖς ταῦτα πᾶσαι;

ΠΑΣΑΙ

                                        νὴ Δία.

ΛΥΣΙΣΤΡΑΤΗ

φέρ᾽ ἐγὼ καθαγίσω τήνδε.

ΚΑΛΟΝΙΚΗ

                                το μέρος γ᾽ ὦ φίλη,
ὅπως ἂν ὦμεν εὐθὺς ἀλλήλων φίλαι.

ΛΑΜΠΙΤΩ

τίς ὠλολυγά;   240

ΛΥΣΙΣΤΡΑΤΗ

                                τοῦτ᾽ ἐκεῖν᾽ οὑγὼ 'λεγον·
αἱ γὰρ γυναῖκες τὴν ἀκρόπολιν τῆς θεοῦ
ἤδη κατειλήφασιν. ἀλλ᾽ ὦ Λαμπιτοῖ
σὺ μὲν βάδιζε καὶ τὰ παρ᾽ ὑμῶν εὖ τίθει,
τασδὶ δ᾽ ὁμήρους κατάλιφ᾽ ἡμῖν ἐνθάδε·
ἡμεῖς δὲ ταῖς ἄλλαισι ταῖσιν ἐν πόλει   245
ξυνεμβάλωμεν εἰσιοῦσαι τοὺς μοχλούς.

ΚΑΛΟΝΙΚΗ

οὔκουν ἐφ᾽ ἡμᾶς ξυμβοηθήσειν οἴει
τοὺς ἄνδρας εὐθύς;

LYSISTRATA
    If I do all this, then I may drink this wine.

CALONICE
    If I do all this, then I may drink this wine.

LYSISTRATA
    If I fail, may this glass fill with water.

CALONICE
    If I fail, may this glass fill with water.

LYSISTRATA
    Do all you women swear this oath?

ALL
                                We do.

LYSISTRATA
    All right. I'll make the offering.

[Lysistrata drinks some of the wine in the bowl]

CALONICE
                        Just your share,
    my dear, so we all stay firm friends.

[A sound of shouting is heard from offstage]

LAMPITO
                    What's that noise?   [240]

LYSISTRATA
    It's what I said just now—the women
    have already captured the Acropolis.
    So, Lampito, you return to Sparta—
    do good work among your people there.
    Leave these women here as hostages.
    We'll go in the citadel with the others
    and help them as they barricade the doors.

CALONICE
    Don't you think the men will band together
    and march against us—and quickly, too.

ΛΥΣΙΣΤΡΑΤΗ

ὀλίγον αὐτῶν μοι μέλει.
οὐ γὰρ τοσαύτας οὔτ᾽ ἀπειλὰς οὔτε πῦρ
ἥξουσ᾽ ἔχοντες ὥστ᾽ ἀνοῖξαι τὰς πύλας   250
ταύτας, ἐὰν μὴ ᾽φ᾽ οἷσιν ἡμεῖς εἴπομεν.

ΚΑΛΟΝΙΚΗ

μὰ τὴν Ἀφροδίτην οὐδέποτέ γ᾽· ἄλλως γὰρ ἂν
ἄμαχοι γυναῖκες καὶ μιαραὶ κεκλήμεθ᾽ ἄν.

ΧΟΡΟΣ ΓΕΡΟΝΤΩΝ

χώρει Δράκης, ἡγοῦ βάδην, εἰ καὶ τὸν ὦμον ἀλγεῖς
κορμοῦ τοσουτονὶ βάρος χλωρᾶς φέρων ἐλάας.   255

— ἦ πόλλ᾽ ἄελπτ᾽ ἔνεστιν ἐν τῷ μακρῷ βίῳ φεῦ,
ἐπεὶ τίς ἄν ποτ᾽ ἤλπισ᾽ ὦ Στρυμόδωρ᾽ ἀκοῦσαι
    γυναῖκας, ἃς ἐβόσκομεν   260
    κατ᾽ οἶκον ἐμφανὲς κακόν,
    κατὰ μὲν ἅγιον ἔχειν βρέτας,
    κατὰ δ᾽ ἀκρόπολιν ἐμὰν λαβεῖν
    μοχλοῖς δὲ καὶ κλήθροισι
        τὰ προπύλαια πακτοῦν;   265

— ἀλλ᾽ ὡς τάχιστα πρὸς πόλιν σπεύσωμεν ὦ Φιλοῦργε,
ὅπως ἄν, αὐταῖς ἐν κύκλῳ θέντες τὰ πρέμνα ταυτί,
ὅσαι τὸ πρᾶγμα τοῦτ᾽ ἐνεστήσαντο καὶ μετῆλθον,
μίαν πυρὰν νήσαντες ἐμπρήσωμεν αὐτόχειρες
πάσας, ὑπὸ ψήφου μιᾶς, πρώτην δὲ τὴν Λύκωνος.   270

— οὐ γὰρ μὰ τὴν Δήμητρ᾽ ἐμοῦ ζῶντος ἐγχανοῦνται·
ἐπεὶ οὐδὲ Κλεομένης, ὃς αὐτὴν κατέσχε πρῶτος,
    ἀπῆθεν ἀψάλακτος, ἀλλ᾽   275

34

LYSISTRATA

    I'm not so worried about them. They'll come
    carrying their torches and making threats,
    but they'll not pry these gates of ours apart,   [250]
    not unless they agree to our demands.

CALONICE

    Yes, by Aphrodite, that's right. If not,
    we'll be labelled weak and gutless women.

*[The women enter the citadel. The Chorus of Old Men enters slowly, for
they are quite decrepit. They are carrying wood for a fire, glowing coals
to start the blaze, and torches to light.]*

LEADER OF MEN'S CHORUS

    Keep moving, Draces, pick up the pace,
    even if your shoulder's tired lugging
    all this heavy fresh-cut olive wood.

CHORUS OF OLD MEN

    Alas, so many unexpected things
    take place in a long life. O Strymodorus,
    who'd ever think they'd hear such news
    about our women—the ones we fed   [260]
    in our own homes are truly bad.
    The sacred statue is in their hands,
    they've seized my own Acropolis
    and block the doors with bolts and bars.

LEADER OF MEN'S CHORUS

    Come on Philurgus, let's hurry there
    as fast as we can go up to the city.
    We'll set these logs down in a circle,
    stack them so we keep them bottled up,
    those women who've combined to do this.
    Then with our own hands we'll set alight
    a single fire and, as we all agreed
    in the vote we took, we'll burn them all,
    beginning first with Lycon's wife.¹⁴   [270]

CHORUS OF OLD MEN

    They'll won't be making fun of me,
    by Demeter, not while I'm still alive.
    That man Cleomenes, who was the first
    to take our citadel, went back unharmed.

ὅμως Λακωνικὸν πνέων
ᾤχετο θὤπλα παραδοὺς ἐμοί,
σμικρὸν ἔχων πάνυ τριβώνιον,
πινῶν ῥυπῶν ἀπαράτιλτος,
   ἐξ ἐτῶν ἄλουτος.   280

οὕτως ἐπολιόρκησ᾽ ἐγὼ τὸν ἄνδρ᾽ ἐκεῖνον ὠμῶς
ἐφ᾽ ἑπτακαίδεκ᾽ ἀσπίδων πρὸς ταῖς πύλαις καθεύδων.
τασδὶ δὲ τὰς Εὐριπίδῃ θεοῖς τε πᾶσιν ἐχθρὰς
ἐγὼ οὐκ ἄρα σχήσω παρὼν τολμήματος τοσούτου;
μή νυν ἔτ᾽ ἐν ⟨τῇ⟩ τετραπόλει τοὐμὸν τροπαῖον εἴη.   285

   ἀλλ᾽ αὐτὸ γάρ μοι τῆς ὁδοῦ
     λοιπόν ἐστι χωρίον
τὸ πρὸς πόλιν τὸ σιμόν, οἷ σπουδὴν ἔχω·
   χὤπως ποτ᾽ ἐξαμπρεύσομεν
     τοῦτ᾽ ἄνευ κανθηλίου.   290
ὡς ἐμοῦ γε τὼ ξύλω τὸν ὦμον ἐξιπώκατον·
   ἀλλ᾽ ὅμως βαδιστέον,
   καὶ τὸ πῦρ φυσητέον,
μή μ᾽ ἀποσβεσθὲν λάθῃ πρὸς τῇ τελευτῇ τῆς ὁδοῦ.
     φῦ φῦ.
     ἰοὺ ἰοὺ τοῦ καπνοῦ.   295

   ὡς δεινὸν ὦναξ Ἡράκλεις
     προσπεσόν μ᾽ ἐκ τῆς χύτρας
ὥσπερ κύων λυττῶσα τὠφθαλμὼ δάκνει·
   κἄστιν γε Λήμνιον τὸ πῦρ
     τοῦτο πάσῃ μηχανῇ.   300
οὐ γὰρ ⟨ἂν⟩ ποθ᾽ ὧδ᾽ ὀδὰξ ἔβρυκε τὰς λήμας ἐμοῦ.
   σπεῦδε πρόσθεν ἐς πόλιν
   καὶ βοήθει τῇ θεῷ.
ἢ πότ᾽ αὐτῇ μᾶλλον ἢ νῦν ὦ Λάχης ἀρήξομεν;
     φῦ φῦ.
     ἰοὺ ἰοὺ τοῦ καπνοῦ.   305

Snorting Spartan pride he went away,
once he'd handed me his weapons,
wearing a really tiny little cloak,
hungry, filthy, with his hairy face.
He'd gone six years without a bath.[15]   [280]

That's how I fiercely hemmed him in,
our men in ranks of seventeen
we even slept before the gates.
So with these foes of all the gods
and of Euripides, as well,
will I not check their insolence?
If I do not, then let my trophies
all disappear from Marathon.[16]

The rest of the journey I have to make
is uphill to the Acropolis.
We must move fast, but how do we haul
this wood up there without a donkey?
This pair of logs makes my shoulders sore.
But still we've got to soldier on
giving our fire air to breathe.
It may go out when I'm not looking
just as I reach my journey's end.

*[They blow on the coals to keep them alight. The smoke comes blowing up in
their faces. The Old Men fall back, coughing and rubbing their eyes]*

O the smoke!
Lord Hercules, how savagely
it jumped out from the pot right in my face
and bit my eyes like a raving bitch.
It works just like a Lemnian fire   [300]
or else it wouldn't use its teeth
to feed on fluids in my eye.
We need to hurry to the citadel
and save the goddess. If not now,
O Laches, when should we help her out?[17]

[The men blow on the coals and are again overpowered by the smoke]

Damn and blast this smoke!

37

— τουτὶ τὸ πῦρ ἐγρήγορεν θεῶν ἕκατι καὶ ζῇ.

οὔκουν ἄν, εἰ τὼ μὲν ξύλω θείμεσθα πρῶτον αὐτοῦ,

τῆς ἀμπέλου δ᾽ ἐς τὴν χύτραν τὸν φανὸν ἐγκαθέντες

ἅψαντες εἶτ᾽ ἐς τὴν θύραν κριηδὸν ἐμπέσοιμεν;

κἂν μὴ καλούντων τοὺς μοχλοὺς χαλῶσιν αἱ γυναῖκες,310

ἐμπιμπράναι χρὴ τὰς θύρας καὶ τῷ καπνῷ πιέζειν.

θώμεσθα δὴ τὸ φορτίον. φεῦ τοῦ καπνοῦ βαβαιάξ.

τίς ξυλλάβοιτ᾽ ἂν τοῦ ξύλου τῶν ἐν Σάμῳ στρατηγῶν;

ταυτὶ μὲν ἤδη τὴν ῥάχιν θλίβοντά μου πέπαυται.

σὸν δ᾽ ἔργον ἐστὶν ὦ χύτρα τὸν ἄνθρακ᾽ ἐξεγείρειν,   315

τὴν λαμπάδ᾽ ἡμμένην ὅπως πρώτιστ᾽ ἐμοὶ προσοίσεις.

δέσποινα Νίκη ξυγγενοῦ τῶν τ᾽ ἐν πόλει γυναικῶν

τοῦ νῦν παρεστῶτος θράσους θέσθαι τροπαῖον ἡμᾶς.

ΧΟΡΟΣ ΓΥΝΑΙΚΩΝ

λιγνὺν δοκῶ μοι καθορᾶν καὶ καπνὸν ὦ γυναῖκες

ὥσπερ πυρὸς καομένου· σπευστέον ἐστὶ θᾶττον.   320

—   πέτου πέτου Νικοδίκη,

πρὶν ἐμπεπρῆσθαι Καλύκην

τε καὶ Κρίτυλλαν περιφυσήτω

ὑπό τε νόμων ἀργαλέων

ὑπό τε γερόντων ὀλέθρων.   325

ἀλλὰ φοβοῦμαι τόδε, μῶν ὑστερόπους βοηθῶ.

νῦν δὴ γὰρ ἐμπλησαμένη τὴν ὑδρίαν κνεφαία

38

LEADER OF MEN'S CHORUS
Thanks to the gods, the fire's up again—
a lively flame. So what if, first of all,
we placed our firewood right down here, then put
a vine branch in the pot, set it alight,
and charged the door like a battering ram?
We'll order women to remove the bars,   [310]
and, if they refuse, we'll burn down the doors.
We'll overpower them with the smoke.
All right, put down your loads.

[The men set down their logs. Once again the smoke is too much for them]

This bloody smoke!
Is there any general here from Samos
who'll help us with this wood?[18]

[He sets down his load of wood]

Ah, that's better.
They're not shrinking my spine any more.
All right, pot, it's now your job to arouse
a fire from those coals, so first of all,
I'll have a lighted torch and lead the charge.
O lady Victory, stand with us here,
so we can set our trophy up in there,
defeat those women in our citadel
put down this present insolence of theirs.

[The Old Men stack their logs in a pile and start lighting their torches on the coals. The Chorus of Old Women enters. They are carrying pitchers of water]

LEADER OF WOMEN'S CHORUS
Ladies, I think I see some flames and smoke,
as if a fire was burning. We'd better hurry.   [320]

CHORUS OF OLD WOMEN
We have to fly, Nicodice, fly
before Critylla is burned up
and Calyce, too, by nasty winds
and old men keen to wipe them out.
But I'm afraid I'll be too late
to help them out. I've only just
filled up my pitcher in the dark.

39

μόλις ἀπὸ κρήνης ὑπ᾽ ὄχλου καὶ θορύβου καὶ πατάγου
   χυτρείου,
   δούλαισιν ὠστιζομένη   330

. . .

   στιγματίαις θ᾽, ἁρπαλέως
   ἀραμένη ταῖσιν ἐμαῖς
   δημότισιν καομέναις
      φέρουσ᾽ ὕδωρ βοηθῶ.

   ἤκουσα γὰρ τυφογέροντας   335
   ἄνδρας ἔρειν, στελέχη
   φέροντας ὥσπερ βαλανεύσοντας
   ἐς πόλιν ὡς τριτάλαντον βάρος,
   δεινότατ᾽ ἀπειλοῦντας ἐπῶν
ὡς πυρὶ χρὴ τὰς μυσαρὰς γυναῖκας ἀνθρακεύειν·   340
ἃς ὦ θεὰ μή ποτ᾽ ἐγὼ πιμπραμένας ἴδοιμι,
ἀλλὰ πολέμου καὶ μανιῶν ῥυσαμένας Ἑλλάδα καὶ
   πολίτας,
   ἐφ᾽ οἷσπερ ὦ χρυσολόφα
   πολιοῦχε σὰς ἔσχον ἕδρας.   345
   καί σε καλῶ ξύμμαχον ὦ
   Τριτογένει᾽, εἴ τις ἐκείνας
   ὑποπίμπρησιν ἀνήρ,
      φέρειν ὕδωρ μεθ᾽ ἡμῶν.

— ἔασον ὦ. τουτὶ τί ἦν; ὦνδρες πόνῳ πόνηροι·   350
οὐ γάρ ποτ᾽ ἂν χρηστοί γ᾽ ἔδρων οὐδ᾽ εὐσεβεῖς τάδ᾽ ἄνδρες.

ΧΟΡΟΣ ΓΕΡΟΝΤΩΝ
   τουτὶ τὸ πρᾶγμ᾽ ἡμῖν ἰδεῖν ἀπροσδόκητον ἥκει·
   ἑσμὸς γυναικῶν οὑτοσὶ θύρασιν αὖ βοηθεῖ.

ΧΟΡΟΣ ΓΥΝΑΙΚΩΝ
   τί βδύλλεθ᾽ ἡμᾶς; οὔ τί που πολλαὶ δοκοῦμεν εἶναι;
   καὶ μὴν μέρος γ᾽ ἡμῶν ὁρᾶτ᾽ οὔπω τὸ μυριοστόν.   355

It was not easy—at the well
the place was jammed and noisy too
with clattering pots, pushy servants,
and tattooed slaves. But I was keen
to carry water to these fires
to help my country's women.

I've heard some dim and dull old men
are creeping here and carrying logs—
a great big load   to our fortress,
as if to warm our public baths.
They're muttering the most awful things
how with their fire they need to turn   [340]
these hateful women into ash.
But, goddess, may I never see
them burned like that—but witness how
they rescue cities, all of Greece,
from war and this insanity.
That's why, golden-crested goddess
who guards our city, these women
now have occupied your shrine.
O Tritogeneia, I summon you
to be my ally—if any man
sets them on fire, help us out
as we carry this water up.[19]

[The Old Men have lit their torches and are about to move against the Acropolis. The Old Women are blocking their way.]

LEADER OF WOMEN'S CHORUS
    Hold on, ladies. What this I see? Men—   [350]
dirty old men—hard at work. Honest types,
useful, god-fearing men, could never do
the things you do.

LEADER OF MEN'S CHORUS
             What's happening here
is something we did not expect to see—
a swarm of women standing here like this
to guard the doors.

LEADER OF WOMEN'S CHORUS
               So you're afraid of us?
Does it look like there's a huge crowd of us?
You're seeing just a fraction of our size—
there are thousands more.

ΧΟΡΟΣ ΓΕΡΟΝΤΩΝ

ὦ Φαιδρία ταύτας λαλεῖν ἐάσομεν τοσαυτί;
οὐ περικατᾶξαι τὸ ξύλον τύπτοντ' ἐχρῆν τιν' αὐταῖς;

ΧΟΡΟΣ ΓΥΝΑΙΚΩΝ

θώμεσθα δὴ τὰς κάλπιδας χἠμεῖς χαμᾶζ', ὅπως ἂν
ἢν προσφέρῃ τὴν χεῖρά τις μὴ τοῦτό μ' ἐμποδίζῃ.

ΧΟΡΟΣ ΓΕΡΟΝΤΩΝ

εἰ νὴ Δί' ἤδη τὰς γνάθους τούτων τις ἢ δὶς ἢ τρὶς   360
ἔκοψεν ὥσπερ Βουπάλου, φωνὴν ἂν οὐκ ἂν εἶχον.

ΧΟΡΟΣ ΓΥΝΑΙΚΩΝ

καὶ μὴν ἰδοὺ παταξάτω τις· στᾶσ' ἐγὼ παρέξω,
κοὐ μή ποτ' ἄλλη σου κύων τῶν ὄρχεων λάβηται.

ΧΟΡΟΣ ΓΕΡΟΝΤΩΝ

εἰ μὴ σιωπήσει, θενών σου 'κκοκκιῶ τὸ γῆρας.

ΧΟΡΟΣ ΓΥΝΑΙΚΩΝ

ἅψαι μόνον Στρατυλλίδος τῷ δακτύλῳ προσελθών.   365

ΧΟΡΟΣ ΓΕΡΟΝΤΩΝ

τί δ' ἢν σποδῶ τοῖς κονδύλοις; τί μ' ἐργάσει τὸ δεινόν;

ΧΟΡΟΣ ΓΥΝΑΙΚΩΝ

βρύκουσά σου τοὺς πλεύμονας καὶ τἄντερ' ἐξαμήσω.

ΧΟΡΟΣ ΓΕΡΟΝΤΩΝ

οὐκ ἔστ' ἀνὴρ Εὐριπίδου σοφώτερος ποιητής·
οὐδὲν γὰρ οὕτω θρέμμ' ἀναιδές ἐστιν ὡς γυναῖκες.

ΧΟΡΟΣ ΓΥΝΑΙΚΩΝ

αἰρώμεθ' ἡμεῖς θοὔδατος τὴν κάλπιν ὦ Ῥοδίππη.   370

LEADER OF MEN'S CHORUS
                    Hey there, Phaedrias!
     Shall we stop her nattering on like this?
     Someone hit her, smack her with a log.

LEADER OF WOMEN'S CHORUS
     Let's put our water jugs down on the ground,
     in case they want to lay their hands on us.
     Down there they won't get in our way.

[The Old Women set down their water jugs]

LEADER OF MEN'S CHORUS
     By god, someone should hit them on the jaw,   [360]
     two or three times, and then, like Boupalus,
     they'll won't have anything much more to say.[20]

LEADER OF WOMEN'S CHORUS
     Come on then—strike me. I'm here, waiting.
     No other bitch will ever grab your balls.

LEADER OF MEN'S CHORUS
     Shut up, or I hit you—snuff out your old age.

LEADER OF WOMEN'S CHORUS
     Try coming up and touching Stratyllis
     with your finger tips!

LEADER OF MEN'S CHORUS
                    What if I thrashed you
     with my fists? Would you do something nasty?

LEADER OF WOMEN'S CHORUS
     With my teeth I'll rip out your lungs and guts!

LEADER OF MEN'S CHORUS
     Euripides is such a clever poet—
     the man who says there's no wild animal
     more shameless than a woman.

LEADER OF WOMEN'S CHORUS
                    Come on then,
     Rhodippe, let's pick up our water jugs.   [370]

[The Old Women pick up their water jugs again]

43

Aristophanes

ΧΟΡΟΣ ΓΕΡΟΝΤΩΝ
τί δ' ὦ θεοῖς ἐχθρὰ σὺ δεῦρ' ὕδωρ ἔχουσ' ἀφίκου;

ΧΟΡΟΣ ΓΥΝΑΙΚΩΝ
τί δαὶ σὺ πῦρ ὦ τύμβ' ἔχων; ὡς σαυτὸν ἐμπυρεύσων;

ΧΟΡΟΣ ΓΕΡΟΝΤΩΝ
ἐγὼ μὲν ἵνα νήσας πυρὰν τὰς σὰς φίλας ὑφάψω.

ΧΟΡΟΣ ΓΥΝΑΙΚΩΝ
ἐγὼ δέ γ' ἵνα τὴν σὴν πυρὰν τούτῳ κατασβέσαιμι.

ΧΟΡΟΣ ΓΕΡΟΝΤΩΝ
τοὐμὸν σὺ πῦρ κατασβέσεις;   375

ΧΟΡΟΣ ΓΥΝΑΙΚΩΝ
                              τοὔργον τάχ' αὐτὸ δείξει.

ΧΟΡΟΣ ΓΕΡΟΝΤΩΝ
οὐκ οἶδά σ' εἰ τῇδ' ὡς ἔχω τῇ λαμπάδι σταθεύσω.

ΧΟΡΟΣ ΓΥΝΑΙΚΩΝ
εἰ ῥύμμα τυγχάνεις ἔχων, λουτρόν ⟨γ'⟩ ἐγὼ παρέξω.

ΧΟΡΟΣ ΓΕΡΟΝΤΩΝ
ἐμοὶ σὺ λουτρὸν ὦ σαπρά;

ΧΟΡΟΣ ΓΥΝΑΙΚΩΝ
                              καὶ ταῦτα νυμφικόν γε.

ΧΟΡΟΣ ΓΕΡΟΝΤΩΝ
ἤκουσας αὐτῆς τοῦ θράσους;

ΧΟΡΟΣ ΓΥΝΑΙΚΩΝ
                              ἐλευθέρα γάρ εἰμι.

ΧΟΡΟΣ ΓΕΡΟΝΤΩΝ
σχήσω σ' ἐγὼ τῆς νῦν βοῆς.

LEADER OF MEN'S CHORUS
Why have you damned women even come here
carrying this water?

LEADER OF WOMEN'S CHORUS
                              And why are you
bringing fire, you old corpse? Do you intend
to set yourself on fire?

LEADER OF MEN'S CHORUS
                        Me? To start a blaze
and roast your friends.

LEADER OF WOMEN'S CHORUS
                          I'm here to douse your fire.

LEADER OF MEN'S CHORUS
You'll put out my fire?

LEADER OF WOMEN'S CHORUS
                            Yes I will. You'll see.

LEADER OF MEN'S CHORUS [*waving his torch*]
I don't know why I'm not just doing it,
frying you in this flame.

LEADER OF WOMEN'S CHORUS
                        Get yourself some soap.
I'm giving you a bath.

LEADER OF MEN'S CHORUS
                          You'll wash me,
you old wrinkled prune?

LEADER OF WOMEN'S CHORUS
                          Yes, it will be
just like your wedding night.

LEADER OF MEN'S CHORUS
                      Listen to her!
She's a nervy bitch!

LEADER OF WOMEN'S CHORUS
                    I'm a free woman.

LEADER OF MEN'S CHORUS
I'll make you shut up!

ΧΟΡΟΣ ΓΥΝΑΙΚΩΝ

ἀλλ' οὐκέθ' ἡλιάζει.   380

ΧΟΡΟΣ ΓΕΡΟΝΤΩΝ

ἔμπρησον αὐτῆς τὰς κόμας.

ΧΟΡΟΣ ΓΥΝΑΙΚΩΝ

σὸν ἔργον ὠχελῷε.

ΧΟΡΟΣ ΓΕΡΟΝΤΩΝ

οἴμοι τάλας.

ΧΟΡΟΣ ΓΥΝΑΙΚΩΝ

μῶν θερμὸν ἦν;

ΧΟΡΟΣ ΓΕΡΟΝΤΩΝ

ποῖ θερμόν; οὐ παύσει; τί δρᾷς;

ΧΟΡΟΣ ΓΥΝΑΙΚΩΝ

ἄρδω σ' ὅπως ἂν βλαστάνῃς.

ΧΟΡΟΣ ΓΕΡΟΝΤΩΝ

ἀλλ' αὖός εἰμ' ἤδη τρέμων.   385

ΧΟΡΟΣ ΓΥΝΑΙΚΩΝ

οὐκοῦν ἐπειδὴ πῦρ ἔχεις, σὺ χλιανεῖς σεαυτόν.

ΠΡΟΒΟΥΛΟΣ

ἆρ' ἐξέλαμψε τῶν γυναικῶν ἡ τρυφὴ
χὠ τυμπανισμὸς χοἰ πυκνοὶ Σαβάζιοι,
ὅ τ' Ἀδωνιασμὸς οὗτος οὑπὶ τῶν τεγῶν,
οὗ 'γώ ποτ' ὢν ἤκουον ἐν τἠκκλησίᾳ;   390
ἔλεγε δ' ὁ μὴ ὥρασι μὲν Δημόστρατος
πλεῖν ἐς Σικελίαν, ἡ γυνὴ δ' ὀρχουμένη

46

LEADER OF WOMEN'S CHORUS
                    You don't judge these things.   [380]

LEADER OF MEN'S CHORUS
    Set her hair on fire!

LEADER OF WOMEN'S CHORUS
                    Get to work, Achelous.²¹

*[She throws her jar of water over the Leader of the Men's Chorus, and,
following the leader's example, the women throw water all over the old
men]*

LEADER OF MEN'S CHORUS
    O, that's bad!

LEADER OF WOMEN'S CHORUS
                    Was that hot enough?

[The women continue to throw water on the old men]

LEADER OF MEN'S CHORUS
                                        Hot enough?
    Won't you stop doing that? What are you doing?

LEADER OF WOMEN'S CHORUS
    I'm watering you to make you bloom.

LEADER OF MEN'S CHORUS
    I'm too old and withered. I'm shaking.

LEADER OF WOMEN'S CHORUS
    Well, you've got your fire. Warm yourselves up.

*[A Magistrate enters with an armed escort of four public guards and
slaves with crowbars and some attendant soldiers]*

MAGISTRATE
    Has not our women's lewdness shown itself
    in how they beat their drums for Sabazius,
    that god of excess, or on their rooftops
    shed tears for Adonis? That's what I heard   [390]
    one time in our assembly. Demostrates—
    what a stupid man he is—was arguing
    that we should sail to Sicily. Meanwhile,
    his wife was dancing round and screaming out

'αἰαῖ Ἄδωνιν' φησίν, ὁ δὲ Δημόστρατος
ἔλεγεν ὁπλίτας καταλέγειν Ζακυνθίων·
ἡ δ' ὑποπεπωκυῖ' ἡ γυνὴ 'πὶ τοῦ τέγους   395
'κόπτεσθ' Ἄδωνιν' φησίν· ὁ δ' ἐβιάζετο
ὁ θεοῖσιν ἐχθρὸς καὶ μιαρὸς Χολοζύγης.
τοιαῦτ' ἀπ' αὐτῶν ἐστιν ἀκόλαστ' ᾄσματα.

ΧΟΡΟΣ ΓΕΡΟΝΤΩΝ
  τί δῆτ' ἂν εἰ πύθοιο καὶ τὴν τῶνδ' ὕβριν;
  αἲ τἄλλα θ' ὑβρίκασι κἀκ τῶν καλπίδων   400
  ἔλουσαν ἡμᾶς, ὥστε θαἰμάτιδια
  σείειν πάρεστιν ὥσπερ ἐνεουρηκότας.

ΠΡΟΒΟΥΛΟΣ
  νὴ τὸν Ποσειδῶ τὸν ἁλυκὸν δίκαιά γε.
  ὅταν γὰρ αὐτοὶ ξυμπονηρευώμεθα
  ταῖσιν γυναιξὶ καὶ διδάσκωμεν τρυφᾶν,   405
  τοιαῦτ' ἀπ' αὐτῶν βλαστάνει βουλεύματα.
  οἳ λέγομεν ἐν τῶν δημιουργῶν τοιαδί·
  'ὦ χρυσοχόε τὸν ορμον ὃν ἐπεσκεύασας,
  ὀρχουμένης μου τῆς γυναικὸς ἑσπέρας
  ἡ βάλανος ἐκπέπτωκεν ἐκ τοῦ τρήματος.   410
  ἐμοὶ μὲν οὖν ἔστ' ἐς Σαλαμῖνα πλευστέα·
  σὺ δ' ἢν σχολάσῃς, πάσῃ τέχνῃ πρὸς ἑσπέραν
  ἐλθὼν ἐκείνῃ τὴν βάλανον ἐνάρμοσον.'
  ἕτερος δέ τις πρὸς σκυτοτόμον ταδὶ λέγει
  νεανίαν καὶ πέος ἔχοντ' οὐ παιδικόν·   415
  'ὦ σκυτοτόμε μου τῆς γυναικὸς τοῦ ποδὸς
  τὸ δακτυλίδιον ξυμπιέζει τὸ ζυγὸν
  ἅθ' ἁπαλὸν ὄν· τοῦτ' οὖν σὺ τῆς μεσημβρίας
  ἐλθὼν χάλασον, ὅπως ἂν εὐρυτέρως ἔχῃ.'
  τοιαῦτ' ἀπήντηκ' ἐς τοιαυτὶ πράγματα,   420
  ὅτε γ' ὢν ἐγὼ πρόβουλος, ἐκπορίσας ὅπως
  κωπῆς ἔσονται, τἀργυρίου νυνὶ δέον,
  ὑπὸ τῶν γυναικῶν ἀποκέκλημαι ταῖς πύλαις.
  ἀλλ' οὐδὲν ἔργον ἑστάναι. φέρε τοὺς μοχλούς,
  ὅπως ἂν αὐτὰς τῆς ὕβρεως ἐγὼ σχέθω.   425

48

"Alas, Adonis!" While Demostrates talked,
saying we should levy soldiers from Zacynthus,
the woman was on the roof top, getting drunk
and yelling out "Weep for Adonis! Weep."[22]
But he kept on forcing his opinion through,
that mad brutal ox, whom the gods despise.
That's just the kind of loose degenerate stuff
that comes from women.

LEADER OF MEN'S CHORUS
                                        Wait until I tell you
the insolent things these women did to us—
all their abuse—they dumped their water jugs   [400]
on us. So now we have to dry our clothes.
We look as if we've pissed ourselves.

MAGISTRATE
                                    By Poseidon,
god of the salt seas, it serves you right.
We men ourselves share in the blame for this.
We teach our wives their free and easy life,
and so intrigues come flowering out from them.
Here's what we tell some working artisan,
"O goldsmith, about that necklace I bought here—
last night my wife was dancing and the bolt   [410]
slipped from its hole. I have to take a boat
to Salamis. If you've got time tonight,
you could visit her with that tool of yours
and fix the way the bolt sits in her hole."
Another man goes to the shoemaker,
a strapping lad with an enormous prick,
and says, "O shoemaker, a sandal strap
is pinching my wife's tender little toe.
Could you come at noon and rub her strap,
stretch it really wide?" That's the sort of thing   [420]
that leads to all this trouble. Look at me,
a magistrate in charge of finding oars
and thus in need of money now—these women
have shut the treasury doors to keep me out.
But standing here's no use.

[He calls out to his two slaves]

                                    Bring the crow bars.
I'll stop these women's insolence myself.

49

τί κέχηνας ὦ δύστηνε; ποῖ δ' αὖ σὺ βλέπεις,
οὐδὲν ποιῶν ἀλλ' ἢ καπηλεῖον σκοπῶν;
οὐχ ὑποβαλόντες τοὺς μοχλοὺς ὑπὸ τὰς πύλας
ἐντεῦθεν ἐκμοχλεύσετ'; ἐνθενδὶ δ' ἐγὼ
ξυνεκμοχλεύσω.   430

ΛΥΣΙΣΤΡΑΤΗ

              μηδὲν ἐκμοχλεύετε·
ἐξέρχομαι γὰρ αὐτομάτη. τί δεῖ μοχλῶν;
οὐ γὰρ μοχλῶν δεῖ μᾶλλον ἢ νοῦ καὶ φρενῶν.

ΠΡΟΒΟΥΛΟΣ

ἄληθες ὦ μιαρὰ σύ; ποῦ 'σθ' ὁ τοξότης;
ξυλλάμβαν' αὐτὴν κὠπίσω τὼ χεῖρε δεῖ.

ΛΥΣΙΣΤΡΑΤΗ

εἴ τἄρα νὴ τὴν Ἄρτεμιν τὴν χεῖρά μοι   435
ἄκραν προσοίσει δημόσιος ὤν, κλαύσεται.

ΠΡΟΒΟΥΛΟΣ

ἔδεισας οὗτος; οὐ ξυναρπάσει μέσην
καὶ σὺ μετὰ τούτου κἀνύσαντε δήσετον;

ΓΥΝΗ Α

εἴ τἄρα νὴ τὴν Πάνδροσον ταύτῃ μόνον
τὴν χεῖρ' ἐπιβαλεῖς, ἐπιχεσεῖ πατούμενος.   440

ΠΡΟΒΟΥΛΟΣ

ἰδού γ' ἐπιχεσεῖ. ποῦ 'στιν ἕτερος τοξότης;
ταύτην προτέραν ξύνδησον, ὁτιὴ καὶ λαλεῖ.

ΓΥΝΗ Β

εἴ τἄρα νὴ τὴν Φωσφόρον τὴν χεῖρ' ἄκραν
ταύτῃ προσοίσεις, κύαθον αἰτήσεις τάχα.

[He turns to the armed guards he has brought with him]

> What are you gaping at, you idiot!
> And you—what are you looking at?
> Why are you doing nothing—just staring round
> looking for a tavern? Take these crowbars
> to the doors there, and then pry them open.
> Come, I'll work to force them with you.

LYSISTRATA *[opening the doors and walking out]*
> No need to use those crowbars. I'm coming out—   [430]
> and of my own free will. Why these crowbars?
> This calls for brains and common sense, not force.

MAGISTRATE
> Is that so, you slut? Where's that officer?
> Seize that woman! Tie her hands!

LYSISTRATA
>   By Artemis,
> he may be a public servant, but if
> he lays a finger on me, he'll be sorry.

MAGISTRATE *[to the first armed guard]*
> Are you scared of her? Grab her round the waist!
> You there, help him out! And tie her up!

OLD WOMAN A[23]
> By Pandrosus, if you lift a hand to her,
> I'll beat you until you shit yourself!   [440]

[The armed guard is so terrified he shits]

MAGISTRATE
> Look at the mess you made! Where is he,
> that other officer?

[The Magistrate turns to a third armed officer]

>   Tie up this one first,
> the one who's got such a dirty mouth.

OLD WOMAN B
> By the god of light, if you just touch her,
> you'll quickly need a cup to fix your eyes.[24]

51

ΠΡΟΒΟΥΛΟΣ

τουτὶ τί ἦν; ποῦ τοξότης; ταύτης ἔχου.   445

παύσω τιν᾽ ὑμῶν τῆσδ᾽ ἐγὼ τῆς ἐξόδου.

ΓΥΝΗ Γ

εἴ τἄρα νὴ τὴν Ταυροπόλον ταύτῃ πρόσει,

ἐκκοκκιῶ σου τὰς στενοκωκύτους τρίχας.

ΠΡΟΒΟΥΛΟΣ

οἴμοι κακοδαίμων· ἐπιλέλοιφ᾽ ὁ τοξότης.

ἀτὰρ οὐ γυναικῶν οὐδέποτ᾽ ἔσθ᾽ ἡττητέα   450

ἡμῖν· ὁμόσε χωρῶμεν αὐταῖς ὦ Σκύθαι

ξυνταξάμενοι.

ΛΥΣΙΣΤΡΑΤΗ

νὴ τὼ θεὼ γνώσεσθ᾽ ἄρα

ὅτι καὶ παρ᾽ ἡμῖν εἰσι τέτταρες λόχοι

μαχίμων γυναικῶν ἔνδον ἐξωπλισμένων.

ΠΡΟΒΟΥΛΟΣ

ἀποστρέφετε τὰς χεῖρας αὐτῶν ὦ Σκύθαι.   455

ΛΥΣΙΣΤΡΑΤΗ

ὦ ξύμμαχοι γυναῖκες ἐκθεῖτ᾽ ἔνδοθεν,

ὦ σπερμαγοραιολεκιθολαχανοπώλιδες,

ὦ σκοροδοπανδοκευτριαρτοπώλιδες,

οὐχ ἕλξετ᾽, οὐ παιήσετ᾽, οὐκ ἀράξετε;

οὐ λοιδορήσετ᾽, οὐκ ἀναισχυντήσετε;   460

παύσασθ᾽, ἐπαναχωρεῖτε, μὴ σκυλεύετε.

[This officer shits his pants and runs off. The Magistrate turns to a fourth officer]

MAGISTRATE
>Who's this here? Arrest her! I'll put a stop
>to all women in this demonstration!

OLD WOMEN C
>By bull-bashing Artemis, if you move
>to touch her, I'll rip out all your hair
>until you yelp in pain.

[The fourth officer shits himself and runs off in terror]

MAGISTRATE
>   This is getting bad.
>There're no officers left. We can't let ourselves   [450]
>be beaten back by women. Come on then,
>you Scythians, form up your ranks.²⁵ Then charge.
>Go at them!

LYSISTRATA
>   By the two goddesses, you'll see—
>we've got four companies of women inside,
>all fighting fit and fully armed.

MAGISTRATE
>   Come on,
>Scythians, twist their arms behind them!

LYSISTRATA *[shouting behind her]*
>Come out here from where you are in there,
>all you female allies, on the double—
>you market women who sell grain and eggs,
>garlic and vegetables, and those who run
>our bakeries and taverns, to the attack!

[Many women emerge from the Acropolis, armed in various ways]

>Hit them, stomp on them, scratch their eyeballs,
>cover them with your abuse! Don't hold back!   [460]

[A general tumult occurs in which the women beat back the Scythian guards]

>That's enough! Back off! Don't strip the armour
>from those you have defeated.

ΠΡΟΒΟΥΛΟΣ

οἴμ᾽ ὡς κακῶς πέπραγέ μου τὸ τοξικόν.

ΛΥΣΙΣΤΡΑΤΗ

ἀλλὰ τί γὰρ ᾤου; πότερον ἐπὶ δούλας τινὰς
ἥκειν ἐνόμισας, ἢ γυναιξὶν οὐκ οἴει
χολὴν ἐνεῖναι;   465

ΠΡΟΒΟΥΛΟΣ

                    νὴ τὸν Ἀπόλλω καὶ μάλα
πολλήν γ᾽, ἐάνπερ πλησίον κάπηλος ᾖ.

ΧΟΡΟΣ ΓΕΡΟΝΤΩΝ

ὦ πόλλ᾽ ἀναλώσας ἔπη πρόβουλε τῆσδε <τῆς> γῆς,
τί τοῖσδε σαυτὸν ἐς λόγους τοῖς θηρίοις συνάπτεις;
οὐκ οἶσθα λουτρὸν οἷον αἵδ᾽ ἡμᾶς ἔλουσαν ἄρτι
ἐν τοῖσιν ἱματιδίοις, καὶ ταῦτ᾽ ἄνευ κονίας;   470

ΧΟΡΟΣ ΓΥΝΑΙΚΩΝ

ἀλλ᾽ ὦ μέλ᾽ οὐ χρὴ προσφέρειν τοῖς πλησίοισιν εἰκῇ
τὴν χεῖρ᾽· ἐὰν δὲ τοῦτο δρᾷς, κυλοιδιᾶν ἀνάγκη.
ἐπεὶ ᾿θέλω ᾿γὼ σωφρόνως ὥσπερ κόρη καθῆσθαι,
λυποῦσα μηδέν᾽ ἐνθαδί, κινοῦσα μηδὲ κάρφος,
ἢν μή τις ὥσπερ σφηκιὰν βλίττῃ με κἀρεθίζῃ.   475

ΧΟΡΟΣ ΓΕΡΟΝΤΩΝ

ὦ Ζεῦ τί ποτε χρησόμεθα τοῖσδε τοῖς κνωδάλοις;
οὐ᾽ γὰρ ἔτ᾽ ἀνεκτὰ τάδε γ᾽, ἀλλὰ βασανιστέον
    τόδε σοι τὸ πάθος μετ᾽ ἐμοῦ
    ὅ τι βουλόμεναί ποτε τὴν   480
    Κραναὰν κατέλαβον, ἐφ᾽ ὅ τι τε
    μεγαλόπετρον ἄβατον ἀκρόπολιν
        ἱερὸν τέμενος.

[The armed women return into the Acropolis]

MAGISTRATE

                          Disaster!
My guards have acted quite disgracefully.

LYSISTRATA
    What did you expect? Did you really think
you were facing a bunch of female slaves?
Or is it your belief that mere women
have no spirit in them?

MAGISTRATE

                   Spirit? By Apollo, yes!
If they're near any man who's got some wine.

LEADER OF MEN'S CHORUS
    In this land you're a magistrate, but here
your words are useless. Why even try
to have a conversation with these bitches?
Don't you know they've just given us a bath
in our own cloaks? And they did not use soap!   [470]

LEADER OF WOMEN'S CHORUS
    Listen, friend. You should never raise your hand
against your neighbour. If you do, then I
will have to punch you in the eye. I'd prefer
to sit quietly at home, like a young girl,
and not come here to injure anyone
or agitate the nest, unless someone
disturbs the hive and makes me angry.

CHORUS OF OLD MEN
    O Zeus, however will we find a way
to deal with these wild beasts? What's going on
is no longer something we can bear.
But we must question them and find out why
they are so angry with us, why they wish   [480]
to seize the citadel of Cranaus,
the holy ground where people do not go,
on the great rock of the Acropolis.[26]

ΧΟΡΟΣ ΓΕΡΟΝΤΩΝ
    ἀλλ᾽ ἀνερώτα καὶ μὴ πείθου καὶ πρόσφερε πάντας
            ἐλέγχους,
    ὡς αἰσχρὸν ἀκωδώνιστον ἐᾶν τὸ τοιοῦτον πρᾶγμα
        μεθέντας.   485

ΠΡΟΒΟΥΛΟΣ
    καὶ μὴν αὐτῶν τοῦτ᾽ ἐπιθυμῶ νὴ τὸν Δία πρῶτα πυθέσθαι,
    ὅ τι βουλόμεναι τὴν πόλιν ἡμῶν ἀπεκλήσατε τοῖσι
        μοχλοῖσιν.

ΛΥΣΙΣΤΡΑΤΗ
    ἵνα τἀργύριον σῶν παρέχοιμεν καὶ μὴ πολεμοῖτε δι᾽ αὐτό.

ΠΡΟΒΟΥΛΟΣ
    διὰ τἀργύριον πολεμοῦμεν γάρ;

ΛΥΣΙΣΤΡΑΤΗ
                        καὶ τἆλλα γε πάντ᾽ ἐκυκήθη.
    ἵνα γὰρ Πείσανδρος ἔχοι κλέπτειν χοἰ ταῖς ἀρχαῖς
            ἐπέχοντες,   490
    ἀεί τινα κορκορυγὴν ἐκύκων. οἱ δ᾽ οὖν τοῦδ᾽ οὕνεκα
            δρώντων
    ὅ τι βούλονται· τὸ γὰρ ἀργύριον τοῦτ᾽ οὐκέτι μὴ καθέλωσιν.

ΠΡΟΒΟΥΛΟΣ
    ἀλλὰ τί δράσεις;

ΛΥΣΙΣΤΡΑΤΗ
                        τοῦτό μ᾽ ἐρωτᾷς; ἡμεῖς ταμιεύσομεν αὐτό.

ΠΡΟΒΟΥΛΟΣ
    ὑμεῖς ταμιεύσετε τἀργύριον;

ΛΥΣΙΣΤΡΑΤΗ
                        τί <δὲ> δεινὸν τοῦτο νομίζεις;
    οὐ καὶ τἄνδον χρήματα πάντως ἡμεῖς ταμιεύομεν
        ὑμῖν;   495

LEADER OF THE MEN'S CHORUS *[to Magistrate]*
So ask her. Don't let them win you over.
Challenge everything they say. If we left
this matter without seeking out the cause
that would be disgraceful.

MAGISTRATE *[turning to Lysistrata]*
Well then, by god,
first of all I'd like to know the reason
why you planned to use these barriers here
to barricade our citadel.

LYSISTRATA
To get your money
so you couldn't keep on paying for war.

MAGISTRATE
Is it money that's the cause of war?

LYSISTRATA
Yes, and all the rest of the corruption.
Peisander and our leading politicians   [490]
need a chance to steal. That's the reason
they're always stirring up disturbances.[27]
Well, let the ones who wish to do this
do what they want, but from this moment on
they'll get no more money.

MAGISTRATE
What will you do?

LYSISTRATA
You ask me that? We'll control it.

MAGISTRATE
You mean
you're going to manage all the money?

LYSISTRATA
You consider that so strange? Isn't it true
we take care of all the household money?

ΠΡΟΒΟΥΛΟΣ
   ἀλλ᾽ οὐ ταὐτόν.

ΛΥΣΙΣΤΡΑΤΗ
            πῶς οὐ ταὐτόν;

ΠΡΟΒΟΥΛΟΣ
                  πολεμητέον ἔστ᾽ ἀπὸ τούτου.

ΛΥΣΙΣΤΡΑΤΗ
   ἀλλ᾽ οὐδὲν δεῖ πρῶτον πολεμεῖν.

ΠΡΟΒΟΥΛΟΣ
                  πῶς γὰρ σωθησόμεθ᾽ ἄλλως;

ΛΥΣΙΣΤΡΑΤΗ
   ἡμεῖς ὑμᾶς σώσομεν.

ΠΡΟΒΟΥΛΟΣ
            ὑμεῖς;

ΛΥΣΙΣΤΡΑΤΗ
            ἡμεῖς μέντοι.

ΠΡΟΒΟΥΛΟΣ
                  σχέτλιόν γε.

ΛΥΣΙΣΤΡΑΤΗ
   ὡς σωθήσει, κἂν μὴ βούλῃ.

ΠΡΟΒΟΥΛΟΣ
            δεινόν ⟨γε⟩ λέγεις.

ΛΥΣΙΣΤΡΑΤΗ
                  ἀγανακτεῖς.
   ἀλλὰ ποιητέα ταῦτ᾽ ἐστὶν ὅμως.   500

ΠΡΟΒΟΥΛΟΣ
            νὴ τὴν Δήμητρ᾽ ἄδικόν γε.

MAGISTRATE
That's not the same.

LYSISTRATA
Why not?

MAGISTRATE
We need the cash
to carry on the war.

LYSISTRATA
Well, first of all,
there should be no fighting.

MAGISTRATE
But without war
how will we save ourselves?

LYSISTRATA
We'll do that.

MAGISTRATE
You?

LYSISTRATA
That's right—us.

MAGISTRATE
This is outrageous!

LYSISTRATA
We'll save you,
even if that goes against your wishes.

MAGISTRATE
What you're saying is madness!

LYSISTRATA
You're angry,
but nonetheless we have to do it.

MAGISTRATE
By Demeter, this is against the law! [500]

59

ΛΥΣΙΣΤΡΑΤΗ
 σωστέον ὦ τᾶν.

ΠΡΟΒΟΥΛΟΣ
  κεἰ μὴ δέομαι;

ΛΥΣΙΣΤΡΑΤΗ
   τοῦδ' οὔνεκα καὶ πολὺ μᾶλλον.

ΠΡΟΒΟΥΛΟΣ
 ὑμῖν δὲ πόθεν περὶ τοῦ πολέμου τῆς τ' εἰρήνης ἐμέλησεν;

ΛΥΣΙΣΤΡΑΤΗ
 ἡμεῖς φράσομεν.

ΠΡΟΒΟΥΛΟΣ
  λέγε δὴ ταχέως, ἵνα μὴ κλάῃς,

ΛΥΣΙΣΤΡΑΤΗ
    ἀκροῶ δή,
 καὶ τὰς χεῖρας πειρῶ κατέχειν.

ΠΡΟΒΟΥΛΟΣ
   ἀλλ' οὐ δύναμαι· χαλεπὸν γὰρ
 ὑπὸ τῆς ὀργῆς αὐτὰς ἴσχειν.   505

ΧΟΡΟΣ ΓΥΝΑΙΚΩΝ
   κλαύσει τοίνυν πολὺ μᾶλλον.

ΠΡΟΒΟΥΛΟΣ
 τοῦτο μὲν ὦ γραῦ σαυτῇ κρώξαις· σὺ δέ μοι λέγε.

ΛΥΣΙΣΤΡΑΤΗ
    ταῦτα ποιήσω.
 ἡμεῖς τὸν μὲν πρότερον πόλεμον καὶ τὸν χρόνον
   ἠνεσχόμεθα
 ὑπὸ σωφροσύνης τῆς ἡμετέρας τῶν ἀνδρῶν ἅττ' ἐποιεῖτε.
 οὐ γὰρ γρύζειν εἰᾶθ' ἡμᾶς. καίτούκ ἠρέσκετέ γ' ἡμᾶς.

LYSISTRATA
My dear fellow, we have to rescue you.

MAGISTRATE
And if I don't agree?

LYSISTRATA
Then our reasons
are that much more persuasive.

MAGISTRATE
Is it true
you're really going to deal with peace and war?

LYSISTRATA
We're going to speak to that.

MAGISTRATE [*with a threatening gesture*]
Then speak fast,
or else you may well start to cry.

LYSISTRATA
Then listen—
and try to keep your fists controlled.

MAGISTRATE
I can't.
I find it difficult to hold my temper.

LEADER OF WOMEN'S CHORUS
It's more likely you're the one who'll weep.

MAGISTRATE
Shut up your croaking, you old bag.

[*To Lysistrata*]
You—talk to me.

LYSISTRATA
I'll do that. Up to now through this long war
we kept silent about all those things
you men were doing. We were being modest.
And you did not allow us to speak up,
although we were not happy. But still,

ἀλλ' ᾐσθανόμεσθα καλῶς ὑμῶν, καὶ πολλάκις ἔνδον ἂν
οὖσαι   510
ἠκούσαμεν ἄν τι κακῶς ὑμᾶς βουλευσαμένους μέγα
πρᾶγμα·
εἶτ' ἀλγοῦσαι τἄνδοθεν ὑμᾶς ἐπανηρόμεθ' ἂν γελάσασαι,
'τί βεβούλευται περὶ τῶν σπονδῶν ἐν τῇ στήλῃ
παραγράψαι
ἐν τῷ δήμῳ τήμερον ὑμῖν;' 'τί δὲ σοὶ ταῦτ';' ἦ δ' ὃς ἂν ἀνήρ.
'οὐ σιγήσει;' κἀγὼ ἐσίγων.

ΓΥΝΗ Β

                                    ἀλλ' οὐκ ἂν ἐγώ ποτ' ἐσίγων.   515

ΠΡΟΒΟΥΛΟΣ

κἂν ᾤμωζές γ', εἰ μὴ 'σίγας.

ΛΥΣΙΣΤΡΑΤΗ

                              τοιγὰρ ἔγωγ' ἔνδον ἐσίγων.
. . . ἕτερόν τι πονηρότερον βούλευμ' ἐπεπύσμεθ' ἂν ὑμῶν·
εἶτ' ἠρόμεθ' ἄν· 'πῶς ταῦτ' ὦνερ διαπράττεσθ' ὧδ' ἀνοήτως;'
ὁ δέ μ' εὐθὺς ὑποβλέψας <ἂν> ἔφασκ', εἰ μὴ τὸν στήμονα
νήσω,
ὀτοτύξεσθαι μακρὰ τὴν κεφαλήν· 'πόλεμος δ' ἄνδρεσσι
μελήσει.'   520

ΠΡΟΒΟΥΛΟΣ

ὀρθῶς γε λέγων νὴ Δί' ἐκεῖνος.

ΛΥΣΙΣΤΡΑΤΗ

                              πῶς ὀρθῶς ὦ κακόδαιμον,
εἰ μηδὲ κακῶς βουλευομένοις ἐξῆν ὑμῖν ὑποθέσθαι;
ὅτε δὴ δ' ὑμῶν ἐν ταῖσιν ὁδοῖς φανερῶς ἠκούομεν ἤδη,
'οὐκ ἔστιν ἀνὴρ ἐν τῇ χώρᾳ;' 'μὰ Δί' οὐ δῆτ',' <εἶφ'> ἕτερός
τις·   524
μετὰ ταῦθ' ἡμῖν εὐθὺς ἔδοξεν σῶσαι τὴν Ἑλλάδα κοινῇ
ταῖσι γυναιξὶν συλλεχθείσαις. ποῖ γὰρ καὶ χρῆν ἀναμεῖναι;

we listened faithfully to you, and often [510]
inside the house we heard your wretched plans
for some great deed. And if we ached inside,
we'd force a smile and simply ask, "Today
in the assembly did the men propose
a treaty carved in stone decreeing peace?"
But our husbands said, "Is that your business?
Why don't you shut up?" And I'd stay silent.

OLD WOMAN
    I'd not have kept my mouth shut.

MAGISTRATE *[to Lysistrata]*
                You'd have been smacked
if you hadn't been quiet and held your tongue.

LYSISTRATA
    So there I am at home, saying nothing.
Then you'd tell us of another project,
even stupider than before. We'd say,
"How can you carry out a scheme like that?
It's foolish." Immediately he'd frown
and say to me, "If you don't spin your thread,
you'll get a major beating on your head. [520]
War is men's concern."

MAGISTRATE
              Yes, by god!
That man spoke the truth.

LYSISTRATA
             You idiot!
Is that sensible—not to take advice
when what you're proposing is so silly?
Then we heard you speaking in the streets,
asking openly, "Are there any men
still left here in our land?" and someone said,
"By god, there's no one." Well then, after that
it seemed to us we had to rescue Greece
by bringing wives into a single group
with one shared aim. Why should we delay?

ἢν οὖν ἡμῶν χρηστὰ λεγουσῶν ἐθελήσητ' ἀντακροᾶσθαι
κἀντισιωπᾶθ' ὥσπερ χἠμεῖς, ἐπανορθώσαιμεν ἂν ὑμᾶς.

ΠΡΟΒΟΥΛΟΣ
ὑμεῖς ἡμᾶς; δεινόν γε λέγεις κοὐ τλητὸν ἔμοιγε.

ΛΥΣΙΣΤΡΑΤΗ
σιώπα.

ΠΡΟΒΟΥΛΟΣ
σοί γ' ὦ κατάρατε σιωπῶ 'γώ, καὶ ταῦτα κάλυμμα
  φορούσῃ   530
περὶ τὴν κεφαλήν; μή νυν ζῴην.

ΛΥΣΙΣΤΡΑΤΗ
ἀλλ' εἰ τοῦτ' ἐμπόδιόν σοι,
  παρ' ἐμοῦ τουτὶ τὸ κάλυμμα λαβὼν
  ἔχε καὶ περίθου περὶ τὴν κεφαλήν,
    κᾆτα σιώπα

ΓΥΝΗ Α
  καὶ τοῦτον τὸν καλαθίσκον.   535

ΛΥΣΙΣΤΡΑΤΗ
  κᾆτα ξαίνειν ξυζωσάμενος
  κυάμους τρώγων·
  πόλεμος δὲ γυναιξὶ μελήσει.

ΧΟΡΟΣ ΓΥΝΑΙΚΩΝ
  αἱρώμεθ' ὦ γυναῖκες ἀπὸ τῶν καλπίδων, ὅπως ἂν
  ἐν τῷ μέρει χἠμεῖς τι ταῖς φίλαισι συλλάβωμεν.   540

ΧΟΡΟΣ ΓΥΝΑΙΚΩΝ
  ἔγωγε γὰρ ⟨ἂν⟩ οὔποτε κάμοιμ' ἂν ὀρχουμένη,
  οὐδὲ τὰ γόνατα κόπος ἕλοι μου καματηρός·
  ἐθέλω δ' ἐπὶ πᾶν ἰέναι
  μετὰ τῶνδ' ἀρετῆς ἕνεχ', αἷς
  ἔνι φύσις, ἔνι χάρις, ἔνι θράσος,   545
  ἔνι δὲ σοφόν, ἔνι ⟨δὲ⟩ φιλόπολις
  ἀρετὴ φρόνιμος.

If you'd like to hear us give some good advice,
then start to listen, keep your mouths quite shut,
the way we did. We'll save you from yourselves.

MAGISTRATE
You'll save us? What you're saying is madness.
I'm not going to put up with it!

LYSISTRATA
                                        Shut up!

MAGISTRATE
Should I shut up for you, you witch, someone   [530]
with a scarf around her head? I'd sooner die!

LYSISTRATA
If this scarf of mine really bothers you,
take it and wrap it round your head. Here—

[Lysistrata takes off her scarf and wraps it over the Magistrate's head.]

Now keep quiet!

OLD WOMAN A
                        And take this basket, too!

LYSISTRATA
Now put on a waist band, comb out wool,
and chew some beans. This business of the war
we women will take care of.

LEADER OF WOMEN'S CHORUS
                                        Come on, women,
get up and leave those jars. It's our turn now   [540]
to join together with our friends.

WOMEN'S CHORUS
With dancing I'll never tire
weariness won't grip my knees
or wear me out. In everything
I'll strive to match the excellence
of these women here—in nature,
wisdom, boldness, charm,
and prudent virtue in the way
they love their country.

ΧΟΡΟΣ ΓΥΝΑΙΚΩΝ

ἀλλ᾽ ὦ τηθῶν ἀνδρειοτάτων καὶ μητριδίων ἀκαληφῶν,
χωρεῖτ᾽ ὀργῇ καὶ μὴ τέγγεσθ᾽· ἔτι γὰρ νῦν οὔρια θεῖτε. 550

ΛΥΣΙΣΤΡΑΤΗ

ἀλλ᾽ ἤνπερ ὅ <τε> γλυκύθυμος Ἔρως χἠ Κυπρογένει᾽
    Ἀφροδίτη
ἵμερον ἡμῶν κατὰ τῶν κόλπων καὶ τῶν μηρῶν
    καταπνεύσῃ,
κᾆτ᾽ ἐντήξῃ τέτανον τερπνὸν τοῖς ἀνδράσι καὶ
    ῥοπαλισμούς,
οἶμαί ποτε Λυσιμάχας ἡμᾶς ἐν τοῖς Ἕλλησι καλεῖσθαι.

ΠΡΟΒΟΥΛΟΣ

τί ποιησάσας;   555

ΛΥΣΙΣΤΡΑΤΗ

            ἢν παύσωμεν πρώτιστον μὲν ξὺν ὅπλοισιν
ἀγοράζοντας καὶ μαινομένους.

ΓΥΝΗ Α

                    νὴ τὴν Παφίαν Ἀφροδίτην.

ΛΥΣΙΣΤΡΑΤΗ

νῦν μὲν γὰρ δὴ κἀν ταῖσι χύτραις κἀν τοῖς λαχάνοισιν
    ὁμοίως
περιέρχονται κατὰ τὴν ἀγορὰν ξὺν ὅπλοις ὥσπερ
    Κορύβαντες.

ΠΡΟΒΟΥΛΟΣ

νὴ Δία· χρὴ γὰρ τοὺς ἀνδρείους.

ΛΥΣΙΣΤΡΑΤΗ

                    καὶ μὴν τό γε πρᾶγμα γέλοιον,
ὅταν ἀσπίδ᾽ ἔχων καὶ Γοργόνα τις κᾆτ᾽ ὠνῆται
    κορακίνους.   560

66

LEADER OF WOMEN'S CHORUS
>You grandchildren of the bravest women,
>sprung from fruitful stinging nettles,
>let your passion drive you forward
>and don't hold back, for now you've got
>the winds of fortune at your back.   [550]

LYSISTRATA
>O Aphrodite born on Cyprus
>and, you, sweet passionate Eros, breathe
>sexual longing on our breasts and thighs
>and fill our men with tortuous desire
>and make their pricks erect. If so, I think
>we'll win ourselves a name among the Greeks
>as those who brought an end to warfare.

MAGISTRATE
>What will you do?

LYSISTRATA
>   For a start, we'll stop
>you men hanging around the market place
>armed with spears and acting up like fools.

OLD WOMAN A
>Yes, that's right, by Paphian Aphrodite!

LYSISTRATA
>Right now in the market they stroll around
>among the pots and vegetables, fully armed,
>like Corybantes.28

MAGISTRATE
>   Yes, that's right—
>it's what brave men should do.

LYSISTRATA
>   It looks so silly—
>going off to purchase tiny little birds
>while carrying a Gorgon shield.29   [560]

67

ΓΥΝΗ Α
νὴ Δί᾽ ἐγὼ γοῦν ἄνδρα κομήτην φυλαρχοῦντ᾽ εἶδον ἐφ᾽
    ἵππου
ἐς τὸν χαλκοῦν ἐμβαλλόμενον πῖλον λέκιθον παρὰ γραός·
ἕτερος δ᾽ <αὖ> Θρᾷξ πέλτην σείων κἀκόντιον ὥσπερ ὁ
    Τηρεύς,
ἐδεδίσκετο τὴν ἰσχαδόπωλιν καὶ τὰς δρυπεπεῖς κατέπινεν.

ΠΡΟΒΟΥΛΟΣ
πῶς οὖν ὑμεῖς δυναταὶ παῦσαι τεταραγμένα πράγματα
    πολλὰ   565
ἐν ταῖς χώραις καὶ διαλῦσαι;

ΛΥΣΙΣΤΡΑΤΗ
                                φαύλως πάνυ.

ΠΡΟΒΟΥΛΟΣ
                                        πῶς; ἀπόδειξον.

ΛΥΣΙΣΤΡΑΤΗ
ὥσπερ κλωστῆρ᾽, ὅταν ἡμῖν ᾖ τεταραγμένος, ὧδε
    λαβοῦσαι,
ὑπενεγκοῦσαι τοῖσιν ἀτράκτοις τὸ μὲν ἐνταυθοῖ τὸ δ᾽
    ἐκεῖσε,
οὕτως καὶ τὸν πόλεμον τοῦτον διαλύσομεν, ἤν τις
    ἐάσῃ,
διενεγκοῦσαι διὰ πρεσβειῶν τὸ μὲν ἐνταυθοῖ τὸ δ᾽
    ἐκεῖσε.   570

ΠΡΟΒΟΥΛΟΣ
ἐξ ἐρίων δὴ καὶ κλωστήρων καὶ ἀτράκτων πράγματα
    δεινὰ
παύσειν οἴεσθ᾽ ὦ ἀνόητοι;

ΛΥΣΙΣΤΡΑΤΗ
                            κἂν ὑμῖν γ᾽ εἴ τις ἐνῆν νοῦς,
ἐκ τῶν ἐρίων τῶν ἡμετέρων ἐπολιτεύεσθ᾽ ἂν ἅπαντα.

ΠΡΟΒΟΥΛΟΣ
πῶς δή; φέρ᾽ ἴδω.

OLD WOMAN A
                              By god,
I myself saw a cavalry commander—
he had long hair and was on horseback—
pouring out some pudding he'd just bought
from an old woman into his helmet.
Another Thracian was waving his spear
and his shield, as well, just like Tereus,
and terrifying the woman selling figs
while gobbling down the ripest ones she had.[30]

MAGISTRATE
    And how will you find the power to stop
    so many violent disturbances
    throughout our states and then resolve them?

LYSISTRATA
    Very easily.

MAGISTRATE
                    But how? Explain that.

LYSISTRATA
    It's like a bunch of yarn. When it's tangled,
    we take it and pass it through the spindle
    back and forth—that's how we'll end the war,
    if people let us try, by sending out   [570]
    ambassadors here and there, back and forth.

MAGISTRATE
    You're an idiot! Do you really think
    you can end such fearful acts with spindles,
    spools, and wool?

LYSISTRATA
                    If you had any common sense,
    you'd deal with everything the way we do
    when we handle yarn.

MAGISTRATE
                    What does that mean?
    Tell me.

69

ΛΥΣΙΣΤΡΑΤΗ

     πρῶτον μὲν ἐχρῆν, ὥσπερ πόκου ἐν βαλανείῳ
ἐκπλύναντας τὴν οἰσπώτην, ἐκ τῆς πόλεως ἐπὶ κλίνης 575
ἐκραβδίζειν τοὺς μοχθηροὺς καὶ τοὺς τριβόλους
    ἀπολέξαι,
καὶ τούς γε συνισταμένους τούτους καὶ τοὺς πιλοῦντας
    ἑαυτοὺς
ἐπὶ ταῖς ἀρχαῖσι διαξῆναι καὶ τὰς κεφαλὰς ἀποτῖλαι·
εἶτα ξαίνειν ἐς καλαθίσκον κοινὴν εὔνοιαν, ἅπαντας
καταμιγνύντας τούς τε μετοίκους κεἴ τις ξένος ἢ φίλος
    ὑμῖν, 580
κεἴ τις ὀφείλει τῷ δημοσίῳ, καὶ τούτους ἐγκαταμεῖξαι·
καὶ νὴ Δία τάς γε πόλεις, ὁπόσαι τῆς γῆς τῆσδ᾽ εἰσὶν
    ἄποικοι,
διαγιγνώσκειν ὅτι ταῦθ᾽ ἡμῖν ὥσπερ τὰ κατάγματα
    κεῖται
χωρὶς ἕκαστον· κᾆτ᾽ ἀπὸ τούτων πάντων τὸ κάταγμα
    λαβόντας
δεῦρο ξυνάγειν καὶ συναθροίζειν εἰς ἕν, κἄπειτα
    ποιῆσαι 585
τολύπην μεγάλην κᾆτ᾽ ἐκ ταύτης τῷ δήμῳ χλαῖναν
    ὑφῆναι.

ΠΡΟΒΟΥΛΟΣ

οὔκουν δεινὸν ταυτὶ ταύτας ῥαβδίξειν καὶ τολυπεύειν,
αἷς οὐδὲ μετῆν πάνυ τοῦ πολέμου;

ΛΥΣΙΣΤΡΑΤΗ

καὶ μὴν ὦ παγκατάρατε
πλεῖν ἤ γε διπλοῦν αὐτὸν φέρομεν, πρώτιστον μέν γε
    τεκοῦσαι
κἀκπέμψασαι παῖδας ὁπλίτας. 590

ΠΡΟΒΟΥΛΟΣ

            σίγα, μὴ μνησικακήσῃς.

ΛΥΣΙΣΤΡΑΤΗ

εἶθ᾽ ἡνίκα χρῆν εὐφρανθῆναι καὶ τῆς ἥβης ἀπολαῦσαι,
μονοκοιτοῦμεν διὰ τὰς στρατιάς. καὶ θἠμέτερον μὲν ἐᾶτε,
περὶ τῶν δὲ κορῶν ἐν τοῖς θαλάμοις γηρασκουσῶν ἀνιῶμαι.

LYSISTRATA

First of all, just as we wash the wool
in a rinsing tub to remove the dirt,
you have to lay the city on a bed,
beat out the rascals, and then drive away
the thorns and break apart the groups of men
who join up together in their factions
seeking public office—pluck out their heads.
Then into a common basket of good will
comb out the wool, the entire compound mix,
including foreigners, guests, and allies,   [580]
anyone useful to the public good.
Bundle them together. As for those cities
which are colonies of this land, by god,
you must see that, as far as we're concerned,
each is a separate skein. From all of them,
take a piece of wool and bring it here.
Roll them together into a single thing.
Then you'll have made one mighty ball of wool,
from which the public then must weave its clothes.

MAGISTRATE

So women beat wool and roll it in balls!
Isn't that wonderful? That doesn't mean
they bear any part of what goes on in war.

LYSISTRATA

You damned fool, of course it does—we endure
more than twice as much as you. First of all,
we bear children and then send them off
to serve as soldiers.

MAGISTRATE

                All right, be quiet.   [590]
Don't remind me of all that.

LYSISTRATA

                    And then,
when we should be having a good time,
enjoying our youth, we have to sleep alone
because our men are in the army.
Setting us aside, it distresses me
that young unmarried girls are growing old
alone in their own homes.

71

Aristophanes

ΠΡΟΒΟΥΛΟΣ

οὔκουν χἄνδρες γηράσκουσιν;

ΛΥΣΙΣΤΡΑΤΗ

μὰ Δί᾽ ἀλλ᾽ οὐκ εἶπας ὅμοιον.
ὁ μὲν ἥκων γάρ, κἂν ᾖ πολιός, ταχὺ παῖδα κόρην
    γεγάμηκεν·   595
τῆς δὲ γυναικὸς σμικρὸς ὁ καιρός, κἂν τούτου μὴ
    ᾽πιλάβηται,
οὐδεὶς ἐθέλει γῆμαι ταύτην, ὀττευομένη δὲ κάθηται.

ΠΡΟΒΟΥΛΟΣ

ἀλλ᾽ ὅστις ἔτι στῦσαι δυνατὸς—

ΛΥΣΙΣΤΡΑΤΗ

σὺ δὲ δὴ τί μαθὼν οὐκ ἀποθνῄσκεις;
χωρίον ἐστί· σορὸν ὠνήσει·   600
μελιτοῦτταν ἐγὼ καὶ δὴ μάξω.
    λαβὲ ταυτὶ καὶ στεφάνωσαι.

ΓΥΝΗ Α

καὶ ταυτασὶ δέξαι παρ᾽ ἐμοῦ.

ΓΥΝΗ Β

καὶ τουτονγὶ λαβὲ τὸν στέφανον.

ΛΥΣΙΣΤΡΑΤΗ

τοῦ δεῖ; τί ποθεῖς; χώρει ᾽ς τὴν ναῦν·   605
    ὁ Χάρων σε καλεῖ,
    σὺ δὲ κωλύεις ἀνάγεσθαι.

ΠΡΟΒΟΥΛΟΣ

εἶτ᾽ οὐχὶ ταῦτα δεινὰ πάσχειν ἔστ᾽ ἐμέ;
νὴ τὸν Δί᾽ ἀλλὰ τοῖς προβούλοις ἄντικρυς
ἐμαυτὸν ἐπιδείξω βαδίζων ὡς ἔχω.   610

72

MAGISTRATE

Don't men get old?

LYSISTRATA

By god, that's not the same at all. For men,
even old ones with white hair, can come back
and quickly marry some young girl. For women
time soon runs out. If they don't seize their chance,
no one wants to marry them—they sit there
waiting for an oracle.

MAGISTRATE

But an old man
who can still get his prick erect . . .

LYSISTRATA *[interrupting]*

O you—

why not learn your lesson and just die? It's time.   [600]
Buy a funeral urn. I'll prepare the dough
for honey cakes.³¹ Take this wreath.

[Lysistrata throws some water over the Magistrate]

OLD WOMAN A

This one, too—
it's from me!

[Old Woman A throws more water on the Magistrate]

OLD WOMAN B

Here, take this garland!

[Old Woman B throws more water on the Magistrate]

LYSISTRATA

Well now,
what do you need? What are you waiting for?
Step aboard the boat. Charon's calling you.
You're preventing him from casting off.³²

MAGISTRATE

I don't have to put up with these insults!
I'll go to the other magistrates, by god,
and show myself exactly as I am!   [620]

73

ΛΥΣΙΣΤΡΑΤΗ

μῶν ἐγκαλεῖς ὅτι οὐχὶ προὐθέμεσθά σε;

ἀλλ᾽ ἐς τρίτην γοῦν ἡμέραν σοὶ πρῲ πάνυ

ἥξει παρ᾽ ἡμῶν τὰ τρίτ᾽ ἐπεσκευασμένα.

ΧΟΡΟΣ ΓΕΡΟΝΤΩΝ

οὐκέτ᾽ ἔργον ἐγκαθεύδειν ὅστις ἔστ᾽ ἐλεύθερος,

ἀλλ᾽ ἐπαποδυώμεθ᾽ ἄνδρες τουτωὶ τῷ πράγματι.   615

ἤδη γὰρ ὄζειν ταδὶ πλειόνων καὶ μειζόνων

    πραγμάτων μοι δοκεῖ,

— καὶ μάλιστ᾽ ὀσφραίνομαι τῆς Ἱππίου τυραννίδος·

καὶ πάνυ δέδοικα μὴ τῶν Λακώνων τινὲς   620

δεῦρο συνεληλυθότες ἄνδρες ἐς Κλεισθένους

τὰς θεοῖς ἐχθρὰς γυναῖκας ἐξεπαίρωσιν δόλῳ

καταλαβεῖν τὰ χρήμαθ᾽ ἡμῶν τόν τε μισθόν,

    ἔνθεν ἔζων ἐγώ.   625

δεινὰ γάρ τοι τάσδε γ᾽ ἤδη τοὺς πολίτας νουθετεῖν,

καὶ λαλεῖν γυναῖκας οὔσας ἀσπίδος χαλκῆς πέρι,

καὶ διαλλάττειν πρὸς ἡμᾶς ἀνδράσιν Λακωνικοῖς,

οἷσι πιστὸν οὐδὲν εἰ μή περ λύκῳ κεχηνότι.

ἀλλὰ ταῦθ᾽ ὕφηναν ἡμῖν ἄνδρες ἐπὶ τυραννίδι.   630

ἀλλ᾽ ἐμοῦ μὲν οὐ τυραννεύσουσ᾽, ἐπεὶ φυλάξομαι

καὶ φορήσω τὸ ξίφος τὸ λοιπὸν ἐν μύρτου κλαδί,

ἀγοράσω τ᾽ ἐν τοῖς ὅπλοις ἑξῆς Ἀριστογείτονι,

ὧδέ θ᾽ ἑστήξω παρ᾽ αὐτόν· αὐτὸς γάρ μοι γίγνεται

τῆς θεοῖς ἐχθρᾶς πατάξαι τῆσδε γραὸς τὴν γνάθον.   635

[The Magistrate exits with his attending slaves]

LYSISTRATA *[calling out to him as he leaves]*
    Are you blaming us for not laying you out
    for burial? Well then, on the third day,
    we'll come and offer up a sacrifice
    on your behalf first thing in the morning.

[Lysistrata and the old women with her return inside the Acropolis]

LEADER OF THE MEN'S CHORUS
    You men, no more sleeping on the job
    for anyone born free! Let's strip ourselves
    for action on this issue. It seems to me
    this business stinks—it's large and getting larger.

[The Old Men strip down, taking almost all their clothes off]

CHORUS OF OLD MEN
    And I especially smelled some gas—
    the tyrant rule of Hippias.
    I've a great fear that Spartan men
    collected here with Cleisthenes,
    have with their trickery stirred up
    these women, whom the gods all hate,
    to seize the treasury and our pay,
    the funds I need to live my way.[33]
    It's terrible these women here
    are thinking about politics
    and prattling on about bronze spears—
    they're women!—and making peace
    on our behalf with Spartan types,
    whom I don't trust, not any more
    than gaping wolves. In this affair,
    those men are weaving plots for us,   [630]
    so they can bring back tyranny.
    But me, I won't give any ground,
    not to a tyrant. I'll stand guard,
    from now on carrying a sword
    inside my myrtle bough. I'll march
    with weapons in the market place
    with Aristogeiton at my side.[34]
    I'll stand with him. And now it's time
    I struck those hostile to gods' law
    and hit that old hag on the jaw.

Aristophanes

ΧΟΡΟΣ ΓΥΝΑΙΚΩΝ

οὐκ ἄρ' εἰσιόντα σ' οἴκαδ' ἡ τεκοῦσα γνώσεται.
ἀλλὰ θώμεσθ' ὦ φίλαι γρᾶες ταδί πρῶτον χαμαί.

— ἡμεῖς γὰρ ὦ πάντες ἀστοὶ λόγων κατάρχομεν
    τῇ πόλει χρησίμων·
εἰκότως, ἐπεὶ χλιδῶσαν ἀγλαῶς ἔθρεψέ με.   640
ἑπτὰ μὲν ἔτη γεγῶσ' εὐθὺς ἠρηφόρουν·
εἶτ' ἀλετρὶς ἦ δεκέτις οὖσα τἀρχηγέτι·
κᾆτ' ἔχουσα τὸν κροκωτὸν ἄρκτος ἦ Βραυρωνίοις·   645
κἀκανηφόρουν ποτ' οὖσα παῖς καλὴ 'χουσ'
    ἰσχάδων ὁρμαθόν·
ἆρα προὐφείλω τι χρηστὸν τῇ πόλει παραινέσαι;
εἰ δ' ἐγὼ γυνὴ πέφυκα, τοῦτο μὴ φθονεῖτέ μοι,
ἢν ἀμείνω γ' εἰσενέγκω τῶν παρόντων πραγμάτων.   650
τοὐράνου γάρ μοι μέτεστι· καὶ γὰρ ἄνδρας ἐσφέρω,
τοῖς δὲ δυστήνοις γέρουσιν οὐ μέτεσθ' ὑμῖν, ἐπεὶ
τὸν ἔρανον τὸν λεγόμενον παππῷον ἐκ τῶν Μηδικῶν
εἶτ' ἀναλώσαντες οὐκ ἀντεσφέρετε τὰς ἐσφοράς,
ἀλλ' ὑφ' ὑμῶν διαλυθῆναι προσέτι κινδυνεύομεν.   655
ἆρα γρυκτόν ἐστιν ὑμῖν; εἰ δὲ λυπήσεις τί με,
τῷδέ γ' ἀψήκτῳ πατάξω τῷ κοθόρνῳ τὴν γνάθον.

ΧΟΡΟΣ ΓΕΡΟΝΤΩΝ

ταῦτ' οὖν οὐχ ὕβρις τὰ πράγματ' ἐστὶ
πολλή; κἀπιδώσειν μοι δοκεῖ τὸ χρῆμα μᾶλλον.   660
ἀλλ' ἀμυντέον τὸ πρᾶγμ' ὅστις γ' ἐνόρχης ἔστ' ἀνήρ.

76

[The Old Men move to threaten the Old Women with their fists]

LEADER OF WOMEN'S CHORUS
    When you get back home, your own mother
    won't know who you are. Come on, old ladies,
    you friends of mine, let's first set our burdens
    on the ground.

WOMEN'S CHORUS
                All you fellow citizens,
    we'll start to give the city good advice
    and rightly, since it raised us splendidly   [640]
    so we lived very well. At seven years old,
    I carried sacred vessels, and at ten
    I pounded barley for Athena's shrine.
    Later as bear, I shed my yellow dress
    for the rites of Brauronian Artemis.
    And once I was a lovely full-grown girl,
    I wore strings of figs around my neck
    and was one of those who carried baskets.[35]
    So I am indebted to the city.
    Why not pay it back with good advice?
    I was born a woman, but don't hold that
    against me if I introduce a plan
    to make our present situation better.   [650]
    For I make contributions to the state—
    I give birth to men. You miserable old farts,
    you contribute nothing! That pile of cash
    which we collected from the Persian Wars
    you squandered. You don't pay any taxes.
    What's more, the way you act so stupidly
    endangers all of us. What do you say?
    Don't get me riled up. I'll take this filthy shoe
    and smack you one right on the jaw.

CHORUS OF OLD MEN
    Is this not getting way too insolent?
    I think it's better if we paid them back.   [660]
    We have to fight this out. So any one
    who's got balls enough to be a man

ἀλλὰ τὴν ἐξωμίδ᾽ ἐκδυώμεθ᾽, ὡς τὸν ἄνδρα δεῖ

ἀνδρὸς ὄζειν εὐθύς, ἀλλ᾽ οὖν ἐντεθριῶσθαι πρέπει.

ἀλλ᾽ ἄγετε λευκόποδες, οἵπερ ἐπὶ Λειψύδριον ἤλθομεν ὅτ᾽

ἦμεν ἔτι,   665

νῦν δεῖ νῦν ἀνηβῆσαι πάλιν κἀναπτερῶσαι

πᾶν τὸ σῶμα κἀποσείσασθαι τὸ γῆρας τόδε.   670

εἰ γὰρ ἐνδώσει τις ἡμῶν ταῖσδε κἂν σμικρὰν λαβήν,

οὐδὲν ἐλλείψουσιν αὗται λιπαροῦς χειρουργίας,

ἀλλὰ καὶ ναῦς τεκτανοῦνται, κἀπιχειρήσουσ᾽ ἔτι

ναυμαχεῖν καὶ πλεῖν ἐφ᾽ ἡμᾶς ὥσπε, Ἀρτεμισία.   675

ἢν δ᾽ ἐφ᾽ ἱππικὴν τράπωνται, διαγράφω τοὺς ἱππέας.

ἱππικώτατον γάρ ἐστι χρῆμα κἄποχον γυνή,

κοὐκ ἂν ἀπολίσθοι τρέχοντος· τὰς δ᾽ Ἀμαζόνας σκόπει,

ἃς Μίκων ἔγραψ᾽ ἐθ᾽ ἵππων μαχομένας τοῖς ἀνδράσιν.

ἀλλὰ τούτων χρῆν ἁπασῶν ἐς τετρημένον ξύλον   680

ἐγκαθαρμόσαι λαβόντας τουτονὶ τὸν αὐχένα.

ΧΟΡΟΣ ΓΥΝΑΙΚΩΝ

εἰ νὴ τὼ θεώ με ζωπυρήσεις,

λύσω τὴν ἐμαυτῆς ὗν ἐγὼ δή, καὶ ποιήσω

τήμερον τοὺς δημότας βωστρεῖν σ᾽ ἐγὼ πεκτούμενον. 685

— ἀλλὰ χἠμεῖς ὦ γυναῖκες θᾶττον ἐκδυώμεθα,

ὡς ἂν ὄζωμεν γυναικῶν αὐτοδὰξ ὠργισμένων.

— νῦν πρὸς ἔμ᾽ ἴτω τις, ἵνα μή ποτε φάγῃ σκόροδα, μηδὲ

κυάμους μέλανας.   690

ὡς εἰ καὶ μόνον κακῶς ἐρεῖς, ὑπερχολῶ γάρ,

αἰετὸν τίκτοντα κάνθαρός σε μαιεύσομαι.   695

78

take off your clothes so we men can smell
the way we should—like men. We should strip.
It's not right to keep ourselves wrapped up.
We're the ones who've got white feet.
We marched to Leipsydrion years ago.[36]
And now let's stand erect again, aroused
in our whole bodies—shake off our old age.   [670]

[The Old Men take off their remaining clothes, hold up their shrivelled phalluses, and threaten the women]

If one of us gives them the slightest chance
there's nothing these women won't continue
trying to work on—building fighting ships,
attacking us at sea like Artemesia.[37]
If they switch to horses, I draw the line.
For women are the best at riding bareback—
their shapely arses do a lovely job.
They don't slip off when grinding at a gallop.
Just look how Micon painted Amazons
fighting men on horseback hand to hand.[38]
So we must take a piece of wood with holes,   [680]
and fit a yoke on them, around their necks.

CHORUS OF OLD WOMEN
By the two goddesses, if you get me roused,
I'll let my wild sow's passion loose and make
you yell to all the people here today
how I'm removing all your hair.

LEADER OF WOMEN'S CHORUS
                                  You ladies,
let's not delay—let's take off all our clothes,
so we can smell a woman's passion
when we're in a ferocious mood.

[The Old Women take off their clothes]

WOMEN'S CHORUS
Now let any man step out against me—
he won't be eating garlic any more,   [690]
and no black beans. Just say something nasty,
I'm so boiling mad, I'll treat you the same way
the beetle did the eagle—smash your eggs.[39]

— οὐ γὰρ ὑμῶν φροντίσαιμ' ἄν, ἢν ἐμοὶ ζῇ Λαμπιτὼ
ἥ τε Θηβαία φίλη παῖς εὐγενὴς Ἰσμηνία.
οὐ γὰρ ἔσται δύναμις, οὐδ' ἢν ἑπτάκις σὺ ψηφίσῃ,
ὅστις ὦ δύστην' ἀπήχθου πᾶσι καὶ τοῖς γείτοσιν.
ὥστε κἀχθὲς θἠκάτῃ ποιοῦσα παιγνίαν ἐγὼ   700
τοῖσι παισὶ τὴν ἑταίραν ἐκάλεσ' ἐκ τῶν γειτόνων,
παῖδα χρηστὴν κἀγαπητὴν ἐκ Βοιωτῶν ἔγχελυν·
οἱ δὲ πέμψειν οὐκ ἔφασκον διὰ τὰ σὰ ψηφίσματα.
κοὐχὶ μὴ παύσησθε τῶν ψηφισμάτων τούτων, πρὶν ἂν
τοῦ σκέλους ὑμᾶς λαβών τις ἐκτραχηλίσῃ φέρων.   705
ἄνασσα πράγους τοῦδε καὶ βουλεύματος,
τί μοι σκυθρωπὸς ἐξελήλυθας δόμων;

ΛΥΣΙΣΤΡΑΤΗ

κακῶν γυναικῶν ἔργα καὶ θήλεια φρὴν
ποιεῖ μ' ἄθυμον περιπατεῖν τ' ἄνω κάτω.

ΧΟΡΟΣ ΓΥΝΑΙΚΩΝ

τί φῄς; τί φῄς;   710

ΛΥΣΙΣΤΡΑΤΗ

ἀληθῆ, ἀληθῆ.

ΧΟΡΟΣ ΓΥΝΑΙΚΩΝ

τί δ' ἐστὶ δεινόν; φράζε ταῖς σαυτῆς φίλαις.

ΛΥΣΙΣΤΡΑΤΗ

ἀλλ' αἰσχρὸν εἰπεῖν καὶ σιωπῆσαι βαρύ.

LEADER OF WOMEN'S CHORUS
>Not that I give a damn for you, not while
>I have Lampito here—Ismenia, too,
>my young Theban friend. You have no power,
>not even with seven times as many votes.
>You're such a miserable old man, even those
>who are you neighbours find you hateful.
>Just yesterday for the feast of Hecate,   [700]
>I planned a party, so I asked my neighbours
>in Boeotia for one of their companions,
>a lovely girl—she was for my children—
>a splendid pot of eels.⁴⁰ But they replied
>they couldn't send it because you'd passed
>another one of your decrees. It doesn't seem
>you'll stop voting in these laws, not before
>someone takes your leg, carries you off
>and throws you out.

[Lysistrata comes out from the Acropolis, looking very worried and angry. The leader of the Women's Chorus addresses her]

>   Here's our glorious leader,
>who does the planning for this enterprise.
>Why have you come here, outside the building,
>and with such a sad expression on your face?

LYSISTRATA
>It's the way these women act so badly,
>together with their female hearts, that makes
>me lose my courage and walk in circles.

LEADER OF WOMEN'S CHORUS
>What are you saying? What do you mean?   [710]

LYSISTRATA
>It's true, so true.

LEADER OF WOMEN'S CHORUS
>   What's wrong? You can tell us—
>we're friends of yours.

LYSISTRATA
>   I'm ashamed to say,
>but it's hard to keep it quiet.

Aristophanes

ΧΟΡΟΣ ΓΥΝΑΙΚΩΝ
μή νύν με κρύψῃς ὅ τι πεπόνθαμεν κακόν.

ΛΥΣΙΣΤΡΑΤΗ
βινητιῶμεν, ᾗ βράχιστον τοῦ λόγου.   715

ΧΟΡΟΣ ΓΥΝΑΙΚΩΝ
ἰὼ Ζεῦ.

ΛΥΣΙΣΤΡΑΤΗ
τί Ζῆν᾽ αὐτεῖς; ταῦτα δ᾽ οὖν οὕτως ἔχει.
ἐγὼ μὲν οὖν αὐτὰς ἀποσχεῖν οὐκέτι
οἷά τ᾽ ἀπὸ τῶν ἀνδρῶν· διαδιδράσκουσι γάρ.
τὴν μέν γε πρώτην διαλέγουσαν τὴν ὀπὴν   720
κατέλαβον ᾗ τοῦ Πανός ἐστι ταὐλίον,
τὴν δ᾽ ἐκ τροχιλείας αὖ κατειλυσπωμένην,
τὴν δ᾽ αὐτομολοῦσαν, τὴν δ᾽ ἐπὶ στρούθου μίαν
ἤδη πέτεσθαι διανοουμένην κάτω
ἐς Ὀρσιλόχου χθὲς τῶν τριχῶν κατέσπασα.   725
πάσας τε προφάσεις ὥστ᾽ ἀπελθεῖν οἴκαδε
ἕλκουσιν. ἤδη γοῦν τις αὐτῶν ἔρχεται.
αὕτη σὺ ποῖ θεῖς;

ΓΥΝΗ Α
                              οἴκαδ᾽ ἐλθεῖν βούλομαι.
οἴκοι γάρ ἐστιν ἔριά μοι Μιλήσια
ὑπὸ τῶν σέων κατακοπτόμενα.

ΛΥΣΙΣΤΡΑΤΗ
                                            ποίων σέων;   730
οὐκ εἶ πάλιν;

ΓΥΝΗ Α
                              ἀλλ᾽ ἥξω ταχέως νὴ τὼ θεὼ
ὅσον διαπετάσασ᾽ ἐπὶ τῆς κλίνης μόνον.

ΛΥΣΙΣΤΡΑΤΗ
μὴ διαπετάννυ, μηδ᾽ ἀπέλθῃς μηδαμῇ.

82

LEADER OF WOMEN'S CHORUS
      Don't hide from me
bad news affecting all of us.

LYSISTRATA
            All right,
I'll keep it short—we all want to get laid.

LEADER OF WOMEN'S CHORUS
O Zeus!

LYSISTRATA
      What's the point of calling Zeus?
There's nothing he can do about this mess.
I can't keep these women from their men,
not any longer—they're all running off.
First I caught one slipping through a hole   [720]
beside the Cave of Pan, then another
trying it with a rope and pulley, a third
deserting on her own, and yesterday
there was a woman on a giant bird
intending to fly down to that place
run by Orsilochus.[41] I grabbed her hair.
They're all inventing reasons to go home.

[A woman come out of the citadel, trying to sneak off]

Here's one of them on her way right now.
Where do you think you're going?

WOMAN A
          Who me?
I want to get back home. Inside the house
I've got bolts of Milesian cloth, and worms
are eating them.

LYSISTRATA
      What worms? Get back in there!   [730]

WOMAN A
I'll come back right away, by god—I just
need to spread them on the bed.

LYSISTRATA
         Spread them?
You won't be doing that. You're not leaving!

ΓΥΝΗ Α

   ἀλλ᾿ ἐῶ 'πολέσθαι τἄρι';

ΛΥΣΙΣΤΡΑΤΗ

               ἢν τούτου δέῃ.

ΓΥΝΗ Β

   τάλαιν᾿ ἐγώ, τάλαινα τῆς Ἀμοργίδος,   735
   ἢν ἄλοπον οἴκοι καταλέλοιφ᾿.

ΛΥΣΙΣΤΡΑΤΗ

                  αὕθ ἡτέρα
   ἐπὶ τὴν Ἄμοργιν τὴν ἄλοπον ἐξέρχεται.
   χώρει πάλιν δεῦρ᾿.

ΓΥΝΗ Β

            ἀλλὰ νὴ τὴν Φωσφόρον
   ἔγωγ᾿ ἀποδείρασ᾿ αὐτίκα μάλ᾿ ἀνέρχομαι.

ΛΥΣΙΣΤΡΑΤΗ

   μή μ᾿ ἀποδείρῃς. ἢν γὰρ ἄρξῃς τοῦτο σύ,   740
   ἑτέρα γυνὴ ταὐτὸν ποιεῖν βουλήσεται.

ΓΥΝΗ Γ

   ὦ πότνι᾿ Εἰλείθυι᾿ ἐπίσχες τοῦ τόκου,
   ἕως ἂν εἰς ὅσιον μόλω 'γὼ χωρίον.

ΛΥΣΙΣΤΡΑΤΗ

   τί ταῦτα ληρεῖς;

ΓΥΝΗ Γ

            αὐτίκα μάλα τέξομαι.

ΛΥΣΙΣΤΡΑΤΗ

   ἀλλ᾿ οὐκ ἐκύεις σύ γ᾿ ἐχθές.

ΓΥΝΗ Γ

               ἀλλὰ τήμερον.   745
   ἀλλ᾿ οἴκαδέ μ᾿ ὡς τὴν μαῖαν ὦ Λυσιστράτη
   ἀπόπεμψον ὡς τάχιστα.

WOMAN A
    My wool just goes to waste?

LYSISTRATA
                    If that's what it takes.

[Woman A trudges back into the Acropolis. Woman B emerges]

WOMAN B
    I'm such a fool, I've left my wretched flax
    back in my house unstripped.

LYSISTRATA
                Another one
    leaving here to go and strip her flax!
    Get back inside!

WOMAN B
              By the goddess of light,
    I'll be right back, once I've rubbed its skin.

LYSISTRATA
    You'll not rub anything. If you start that,   [740]
    some other woman will want to do the same.

[Woman B returns dejected into the citadel. Woman C emerges from the citadel, looking very pregnant]

WOMAN C
    O sacred Eileithia, goddess of birth,
    hold back my labour pains till I can find
    a place where I'm permitted to give birth.[42]

LYSISTRATA
    What are you moaning about?

WOMAN C
                  It's my time—
    I'm going to have a child!

LYSISTRATA
              But yesterday
    you weren't even pregnant.

WOMAN C
             Well, today I am.
    Send me home, Lysistrata, and quickly.
    I need a midwife.

ΛΥΣΙΣΤΡΑΤΗ

     τίνα λόγον λέγεις;
τί τοῦτ᾽ ἔχεις τὸ σκληρόν;

ΓΥΝΗ Γ

      ἄρεν παιδίον.

ΛΥΣΙΣΤΡΑΤΗ

μὰ τὴν Ἀφροδίτην οὐ σύ γ᾽, ἀλλ᾽ ἢ χαλκίον
ἔχειν τι φαίνει κοῖλον· εἴσομαι δ᾽ ἐγώ.   750
ὦ καταγέλαστ᾽ ἔχουσα τὴν ἱερὰν κυνῆν
κυεῖν ἔφασκες;

ΓΥΝΗ Γ

     καὶ κυῶ γε νὴ Δία.

ΛΥΣΙΣΤΡΑΤΗ

τί δῆτα ταύτην εἶχες;

ΓΥΝΗ Γ

      ἵνα μ᾽ εἰ καταλάβοι
ὁ τόκος ἔτ᾽ ἐν πόλει, τέκοιμ᾽ ἐς τὴν κυνῆν
ἐσβᾶσα ταύτην, ὥσπερ αἱ περιστεραί.   755

ΛΥΣΙΣΤΡΑΤΗ

τί λέγεις; προφασίζει· περιφανῆ τὰ πράγματα.
οὐ τἀμφιδρόμια τῆς κυνῆς αὐτοῦ μενεῖς;

ΓΥΝΗ Γ

ἀλλ᾽ οὐ δύναμαι 'γωγ᾽ οὐδὲ κοιμᾶσθ᾽ ἐν πόλει,
ἐξ οὗ τὸν ὄφιν εἶδον τὸν οἰκουρόν ποτε.

ΓΥΝΗ Δ

ἐγὼ δ᾽ ὑπὸ τῶν γλαυκῶν γε τάλαιν᾽ ἀπόλλυμαι   760
ταῖς ἀγρυπνίαισι κακκαβαζουσῶν ἀεί.

LYSISTRATA *[inspecting Woman C's clothing]*
                        What are you saying?
What's this you've got here? It feels quite rigid.

WOMAN C
    A little boy.

LYSISTRATA
                        No, by Aphrodite,
    I don't think so. It looks like you've got   [750]
    some hollow metal here. I'll have a look.

[Lysistrata looks under the woman's dress and pulls out a helmet]

    You silly creature, you've got a helmet there,
    Athena's sacred helmet. Didn't you say
    you were pregnant.

WOMAN C
                        Yes, and by god, I am.

LYSISTRATA
    Then why've you got this helmet?

WOMAN C
                        Well, in case
    I went into labour in the citadel.
    I could give birth right in the helmet,
    lay it in there like a nesting pigeon.

LYSISTRATA
    What are you talking about? You're just
    making an excuse—that's so obvious.
    You'll stay here for at least five days
    until your new child's birth is purified.

WOMAN C
    I can't get any sleep in the Acropolis,
    not since I saw the snake that guards the place.

[More women start sneaking out of the citadel]

WOMAN D
    Nor can I. I'm dying from lack of sleep   [760]
    those wretched owls keep hooting all the time.

Aristophanes

ΛΥΣΙΣΤΡΑΤΗ
ὦ δαιμόνιαι παύσασθε τῶν τερατευμάτων.
ποθεῖτ᾽ ἴσως τοὺς ἄνδρας· ἡμᾶς δ᾽ οὐκ οἴει
ποθεῖν ἐκείνους; ἀργαλέας γ᾽ εὖ οἶδ᾽ ὅτι
ἄγουσι νύκτας. ἀλλ᾽ ἀνάσχεσθ᾽ ὦγαθαί,   765
καὶ προσταλαιπωρήσατ᾽ ἔτ᾽ ὀλίγον χρόνον,
ὡς χρησμὸς ἡμῖν ἐστιν ἐπικρατεῖν, ἐὰν
μὴ στασιάσωμεν· ἔστι δ᾽ ὁ χρησμὸς οὑτοσί.

ΓΥΝΗ Α
λέγ᾽ αὐτὸν ἡμῖν ὅ τι λέγει.

ΛΥΣΙΣΤΡΑΤΗ
                σιγᾶτε δή.
ἀλλ᾽ ὁπόταν πτήξωσι χελιδόνες εἰς ἕνα χῶρον,   770
τοὺς ἔποπας φεύγουσαι, ἀπόσχωνταί τε φαλήτων,
παῦλα κακῶν ἔσται, τὰ δ᾽ ὑπέρτερα νέρτερα θήσει
Ζεὺς ὑψιβρεμέτης—

ΓΥΝΗ Β
                ἐπάνω κατακεισόμεθ᾽ ἡμεῖς;

ΛΥΣΙΣΤΡΑΤΗ
ἢν δὲ διαστῶσιν καὶ ἀναπτῶνται πτερύγεσσιν
ἐξ ἱεροῦ ναοῖο χελιδόνες, οὐκέτι δόξει   775
ὄρνεον οὐδ᾽ ὁτιοῦν καταπυγωνέστερον εἶναι.

ΓΥΝΗ Α
σαφής γ᾽ ὁ χρησμὸς νὴ Δί᾽.

ΛΥΣΙΣΤΡΑΤΗ
                ὦ πάντες θεοί,
μή νυν ἀπείπωμεν ταλαιπωρούμεναι,
ἀλλ᾽ εἰσίωμεν. καὶ γὰρ αἰσχρὸν τουτογὶ
ὦ φίλταται, τὸν χρησμὸν εἰ προδώσομεν.   780

ΧΟΡΟΣ ΓΕΡΟΝΤΩΝ
μῦθον βούλομαι λέξαι τιν᾽ ὑμῖν, ὅν ποτ᾽ ἤκουσ᾽
αὐτὸς ἔτι παῖς ὤν.

88

LYSISTRATA

>Come on ladies, stop all these excuses!
>All right, you miss your men. But don't you see
>they miss you, too? I'm sure the nights they spend
>don't bring them any pleasure. But please, dear friends,
>hold on—persevere a little longer.
>An oracle has said we will prevail,
>if we stand together. That's what it said.

WOMAN A

>Tell us what it prophesied.

LYSISTRATA

>   Then, keep quiet.
>"When the sparrows, as they fly away,   [770]
>escaping from the hoopoe birds, shall stay
>together in one place and shall say nay
>to sexual encounters, then a bad day
>will be rare. High thundering Zeus will say
>'What once was underneath on top I'll lay.'"

WOMAN B [*interrupting*]

>Women are going to lie on top of men?

LYSISTRATA [*continuing the oracle*]

>" . . . but if the sparrows fight and fly away
>out of the holy shrine, people will say
>no bird is more promiscuous than they."

WOMAN A

>That oracle is clear enough, by god.

LYSISTRATA

>All you heavenly gods, can we stop talking
>of being in such distress. Let us go back in.
>For, my dearest friends, it will be a shame
>if we don't live up to this prophecy.   [780]

[*Lysistrata and the women go back into the citadel, leaving the two choruses*]

MEN'S CHORUS

>I'd like to tell you all a tale,
>which I heard once when I was young

οὕτως ἦν νεανίσκος Μελανίων τις,   785
ὃς φεύγων γάμον ἀφίκετ' ἐς ἐρημίαν,
κἂν τοῖς ὄρεσιν ᾤκει·
κᾆτ' ἐλαγοθήρει
πλεξάμενος ἄρκυς,   790
καὶ κύνα τιν' εἶχεν,
κοὐκέτι κατῆλθε πάλιν οἴκαδ' ὑπὸ μίσους.
οὕτω τὰς γυναῖκας ἐβδελύχθη
'κεῖνος, ἡμεῖς τ' οὐδὲν ἧττον   795
τοῦ Μελανίωνος οἱ σώφρονες.

ΓΕΡΩΝ

βούλομαί σε γραῦ κύσαι—

ΓΥΝΗ

κρόμμυόν τἄρ' οὐκ ἔδει.

ΓΕΡΩΝ

κἀνατείνας λακτίσαι.

ΓΥΝΗ

τὴν λόχμην πολλὴν φορεῖς.   800

ΧΟΡΟΣ ΓΕΡΟΝΤΩΝ

καὶ Μυρωνίδης γὰρ ἦν
τραχὺς ἐντεῦθεν μελάμπυγός
τε τοῖς ἐχθροῖς ἅπασιν,
ὥς δὲ καὶ Φορμίων.

ΧΟΡΟΣ ΓΥΝΑΙΚΩΝ

κἀγὼ βούλομαι μῦθόν τιν' ὑμῖν ἀντιλέξαι   805
τῷ Μελανίωνι.
Τίμων ἦν ἀΐδρυτός τις ἀβάτοισιν
ἐν σκώλοισι τὸ πρόσωπον περιειργμένος,   810
Ἐρινύων ἀπορώξ.
οὗτος οὖν ὁ Τίμων

. . .

ᾤχεθ' ὑπὸ μίσους
πολλὰ καταρασάμενος ἀνδράσι πονηροῖς.   815

about Melanion, a lad
who fled from marriage and then came
into the wilds and so he lived
up in the hills. He wove some nets   [790]
and hunted hares. He had a dog.
Not once did he return back home
He hated women   they made him sick.
And we are no less wise than he.

LEADER OF MEN'S CHORUS

Let's kiss, old bag, give it a try.

LEADER OF WOMEN'S CHORUS

You won't need onions to make you cry.

LEADER OF MEN'S CHORUS

I'll lift my leg—give you a kick.

LEADER OF WOMAN'S CHORUS

Down there your pubic hair's too thick.   [800]

LEADER OF MEN'S CHORUS

Myronides had a hairy dick
and beat foes with his big black bum.
That Phormio was another one.43

WOMEN'S CHORUS

To you I'd like to tell a tale
to answer your Melanion.
There was a man called Timon once,
a vagabond, the Furies' child.
Wild thistles covered his whole face.   [810]
He wandered off filled up with spite
and always cursing evil types.

οὕτω 'κεῖνος ὑμῶν ἀντεμίσει
τοὺς πονηροὺς ἄνδρας ἀεί,
ταῖσι δὲ γυναιξὶν ἦν φίλτατος.   820

ΓΥΝΗ

τὴν γνάθον βούλει θένω;

ΓΕΡΩΝ

μηδαμῶς· ἔδεισά γε.

ΓΥΝΗ

ἀλλὰ κρούσω τῷ σκέλει;

ΓΕΡΩΝ

τὸν σάκανδρον ἐκφανεῖς.

ΧΟΡΟΣ ΓΥΝΑΙΚΩΝ

ἀλλ' ὅμως ἂν οὐκ ἴδοις   825
καίπερ οὔσης γραὸς ὄντ' αὐτὸν
κομήτην, ἀλλ' ἀπεψιλωμένον
τῷ λύχνῳ.

ΛΥΣΙΣΤΡΑΤΗ
ἰοὺ ἰοὺ γυναῖκες ἴτε δεῦρ' ὡς ἐμὲ
ταχέως.

ΚΑΛΟΝΙΚΗ

τί δ' ἔστιν; εἰπέ μοι τίς ἡ βοή;   830

ΛΥΣΙΣΤΡΑΤΗ
ἄνδρ' ⟨ἄνδρ'⟩ ὁρῶ προσιόντα παραπεπληγμένον,
τοῖς τῆς Ἀφροδίτης ὀργίοις εἰλημμένον.
ὦ πότνια Κύπρου καὶ Κυθήρων καὶ Πάφου
μεδέουσ', ἴθ' ὀρθὴν ἥνπερ ἔρχι τὴν ὁδόν.

ΚΑΛΟΝΙΚΗ
ποῦ δ' ἐστὶν ὅστις ἐστί;   835

ΛΥΣΙΣΤΡΑΤΗ

παρὰ τὸ τῆς Χλόης.

But though he always hated men,
those of you who are such rogues,
women he always really loved.   [820]

LEADER OF WOMEN'S CHORUS
  You'd like a punch right on the chin?

LEADER OF MEN'S CHORUS
  Not given the state of fear I'm in.

LEADER OF WOMEN'S CHORUS
  What if I kicked you with my toe?

LEADER OF MEN'S CHORUS
  We'd see your pussy down below.

LEADER OF WOMEN'S CHORUS
  And then you'd see, although I'm old
  it's not all matted hair down there,
  but singed by lamp and plucked with flair.

*[Lysistrata appears on a balcony of the citadel, looking off in the distance.
Other women come out after her]*

LYSISTRATA
  Hey, you women! Over here to me. Come quick!

CALONICE
  What's going on? Why are you shouting?   [830]

LYSISTRATA
                A man!
  I see a man approaching mad with love,
  seized with desire for Aphrodite's rites.
  O holy queen of Cyprus, Cythera,
  and Paphos, keep moving down the road,
  the straight path you've been travelling on.

CALONICE
  Where is he, whoever he is?

LYSISTRATA
              Over there,
  right beside the shrine of Chloe.

ΚΑΛΟΝΙΚΗ

ὢ νὴ Δί᾽ ἔστι δῆτα. τίς κἀστίν ποτε;

ΛΥΣΙΣΤΡΑΤΗ

ὁρᾶτε· γιγνώσκει τις ὑμῶν;

ΜΥΡΡΙΝΗ

νὴ Δία
ἔγωγε· κἀστὶν οὑμὸς ἀνὴρ Κινησίας.

ΛΥΣΙΣΤΡΑΤΗ

σὸν ἔργον ἤδη τοῦτον ὀπτᾶν καὶ στρέφειν
κἀξηπεροπεύειν καὶ φιλεῖν καὶ μὴ φιλεῖν,   840
καὶ πάνθ᾽ ὑπέχειν πλὴν ὧν σύνοιδεν ἡ κύλιξ.

ΜΥΡΡΙΝΗ

ἀμέλει ποιήσω ταῦτ᾽ ἐγώ.

ΛΥΣΙΣΤΡΑΤΗ

καὶ μὴν ἐγὼ
ξυνηπεροπεύσω ⟨σοι⟩ παραμένουσ᾽ ἐνθαδί,
καὶ ξυσταθεύσω τοῦτον. ἀλλ᾽ ἀπέλθετε.

ΚΙΝΗΣΙΑΣ

οἴμοι κακοδαίμων, οἷος ὁ σπασμός μ᾽ ἔχει   845
χὠ τέτανος ὥσπερ ἐπὶ τροχοῦ στρεβλούμενον.

ΛΥΣΙΣΤΡΑΤΗ

τίς οὗτος οὑντὸς τῶν φυλάκων ἑστώς;

ΚΙΝΗΣΙΑΣ

ἐγώ.

ΛΥΣΙΣΤΡΑΤΗ

ἀνήρ;

CALONICE
                              Oh yes,
   there he is, by god. Who is he?

LYSISTRATA
                        Have a look.
   Do any of you know him?

MYRRHINE
                              O god, I do.
   It's my husband Cinesias.

LYSISTRATA
                                 All right,
   your job is to torment him, be a tease,
   make him hot, offer to have sex with him   [840]
   and then refuse, try everything you can,
   except the things you swore to on the cup.

MYRRHINE
   Don't you worry. I'll do that.

LYSISTRATA
                                 All right, then.
   I'll stay here to help you play with him.
   We'll warm him up together. You others,
   go inside.

*[The women go inside, including Myrrhine. Cinesias enters with a very
large erection. An attendant comes with him carrying a young baby]*

CINESIAS
                           I'm in a dreadful way.
   It's all this throbbing. And the strain. I feel
   as if I'm stretched out on the rack.

LYSISTRATA
                                 Who's there,
   standing inside our line of sentinels?

CINESIAS
   It's me.

LYSISTRATA
             A man?

95

ΚΙΝΗΣΙΑΣ
  ἀνὴρ δῆτ'.

ΛΥΣΙΣΤΡΑΤΗ
      οὐκ ἄπει δῆτ' ἐκποδών;

ΚΙΝΗΣΙΑΣ
  σὺ δ' εἶ τίς ἠκβάλλουσά μ';

ΛΥΣΙΣΤΡΑΤΗ
          ἡμεροσκόπος.

ΚΙΝΗΣΙΑΣ
  πρὸς τῶν θεῶν νυν ἐκκάλεσόν μοι Μυρίνην.   850

ΛΥΣΙΣΤΡΑΤΗ
  ἰδοὺ καλέσω 'γὼ Μυρίνην σοι; σὺ δὲ τίς εἶ;

ΚΙΝΗΣΙΑΣ
  ἀνὴρ ἐκείνης, Παιονίδης Κινησίας.

ΛΥΣΙΣΤΡΑΤΗ
  ὦ χαῖρε φίλτατ'· οὐ γὰρ ἀκλεὲς τοὔνομ
  τὸ σὸν παρ' ἡμῖν ἐστιν οὐδ' ἀνώνυμον.
  ἀεὶ γὰρ ἡ γυνή σ' ἔχει διὰ στόμα.   855
  κἂν ᾠὸν ἢ μῆλον λάβῃ, 'Κινησίᾳ
  τουτὶ γένοιτο,' φησίν.

ΚΙΝΗΣΙΑΣ
  ὦ πρὸς τῶν θεῶν.

ΛΥΣΙΣΤΡΑΤΗ
  νὴ τὴν Ἀφροδίτην· κἂν περὶ ἀνδρῶν γ' ἐμπέσῃ
  λόγος τις, εἴρηκ' εὐθέως ἡ σὴ γυνὴ
  ὅτι λῆρός ἐστι τἄλλα πρὸς Κινησίαν.   860

ΚΙΝΗΣΙΑΣ
  ἴθι νυν κάλεσον αὐτήν.

CINESIAS

Yes, take a look at this!

LYSISTRATA

In that case leave. Go on your way.

CINESIAS

Who are you
to tell me to get out?

LYSISTRATA

The daytime watch.

CINESIAS

Then, by the gods, call Myrrhine for me.   [850]

LYSISTRATA

You tell me to summon Myrrhine for you?
Who are you?

CINESIAS

Cinesias, her husband,
from Paeonidae.[44]

LYSISTRATA

Welcome, dear friend, your name
is not unknown to us. Your wife always
has you on her lips. Any time she licks
an apple or an egg she says, "Ah me,
if only this could be Cinesias."

[Lysistrata licks her fist obscenely]

CINESIAS

O my god!

LYSISTRATA

Yes, by Aphrodite, yes. And when our talk
happens to deal with men, your wife speaks up
immediately, "O they're all useless sorts   [860]
compared to my Cinesias."

CINESIAS

Please call her out.

97

ΛΥΣΙΣΤΡΑΤΗ

τί οὖν; δώσεις τί μοι;

ΚΙΝΗΣΙΑΣ

ἔγωγέ ⟨σοι⟩ νὴ τὸν Δί᾽, ἢν βούλῃ γε σύ·
ἔχω δὲ τοῦθ᾽· ὅπερ οὖν ἔχω, δίδωμί σοι.

ΛΥΣΙΣΤΡΑΤΗ

φέρε νυν καλέσω καταβᾶσά σοι.

ΚΙΝΗΣΙΑΣ

ταχύ νυν πάνυ.

ὡς οὐδεμίαν ἔχω γε τῷ βίῳ χάριν,   865
ἐξ οὗπερ αὕτη 'ξῆλθεν ἐκ τῆς οἰκίας·
ἀλλ᾽ ἄχθομαι μὲν εἰσιών, ἔρημα δὲ
εἶναι δοκεῖ μοι πάντα, τοῖς δὲ σιτίοις
χάριν οὐδεμίαν οἶδ᾽ ἐσθίων· ἔστυκα γάρ.

ΜΥΡΡΙΝΗ

φιλῶ φιλῶ 'γὼ τοῦτον· ἀλλ᾽ οὐ βούλεται   870
ὑπ᾽ ἐμοῦ φιλεῖσθαι. σὺ δ᾽ ἐμὲ τούτῳ μὴ κάλει.

ΚΙΝΗΣΙΑΣ

ὦ γλυκύτατον Μυρινίδιον τί ταῦτα δρᾷς;
κατάβηθι δεῦρο.

ΜΥΡΡΙΝΗ

μὰ Δί᾽ ἐγὼ μὲν αὐτόσ᾽ οὔ.

ΚΙΝΗΣΙΑΣ

ἐμοῦ καλοῦντος οὐ καταβήσει Μυρίνη;

ΜΥΡΡΙΝΗ

οὐ γὰρ δεόμενος οὐδὲν ἐκκαλεῖς ἐμέ.   875

98

LYSISTRATA
> Why should I do that? What will you give me?

CINESIAS
> Whatever you want, by god. I have this . . .

[Cinesias waves his erection in front of Lysistrata]

> I'll give you what I've got.

LYSISTRATA
>   No thanks.
> I think I'll tell her to come out to you.

[Lysistrata leaves to fetch Myrrhine]

CINESIAS
> Hurry up. I've had no pleasure in life
> since she's been gone from home. I go out,
> but I'm in pain. To me now everything
> seems empty. There's no joy in eating food.
> I'm just so horny.

[Lysistrata appears dragging Myrrhine with her. Myrrhine is pretending to be reluctant]

MYRRHINE *[loudly so that Cinesias can hear]*
>   I love him. I do.
> But he's unwilling to make love to me,   [870]
> to love me back. Don't make me go to him.

CINESIAS
> O my dear sweetest little Myrrhine,
> what are you doing? Come down here.

MYRRHINE
> I'm not going there, by god.

CINESIAS
>   If I ask you,
> won't you come down, Myrrhine?

MYRRHINE
> You've got no reason to be calling me.
> You don't want me.

99

ΚΙΝΗΣΙΑΣ

ἐγὼ οὐ δεόμενος; ἐπιτετριμμένος μὲν οὖν.

ΜΥΡΡΙΝΗ

ἄπειμι.

ΚΙΝΗΣΙΑΣ

μὴ δῆτ᾽, ἀλλὰ τῷ γοῦν παιδίῳ
ὑπάκουσον· οὗτος οὐ καλεῖς τὴν μαμμίαν;

ΠΑΙΣ

μαμμία, μαμμία, μαμμία.

ΚΙΝΗΣΙΑΣ

αὕτη τί πάσχεις; οὐδ᾽ ἐλεεῖς τὸ παιδίον   880
ἄλουτον ὂν κἄθηλον ἕκτην ἡμέραν;

ΜΥΡΡΙΝΗ

ἔγωγ᾽ ἐλεῶ δῆτ᾽· ἀλλ᾽ ἀμελὴς αὐτῷ πατὴρ
ἔστιν.

ΚΙΝΗΣΙΑΣ

κατάβηθ᾽ ὦ δαιμονία τῷ παιδίῳ.

ΜΥΡΡΙΝΗ

οἷον τὸ τεκεῖν· καταβατέον. τί γὰρ πάθω;

ΚΙΝΗΣΙΑΣ

ἐμοὶ γὰρ αὕτη καὶ νεωτέρα δοκεῖ   885
πολλῷ γεγενῆσθαι κἀγανώτερον βλέπειν·
χἀ δυσκολαίνει πρὸς ἐμὲ καὶ βρενθύεται,
ταῦτ᾽ αὐτὰ δή 'σθ᾽ ἃ κἄμ᾽ ἐπιτρίβει τῷ πόθῳ.

ΜΥΡΡΙΝΗ

ὦ γλυκύτατον σὺ τεκνίδιον κακοῦ πατρός,
φέρε σε φιλήσω γλυκύτατον τῇ μαμμίᾳ.   890

CINESIAS
　　　　　You don't think I want you?
　I'm absolutely dying for you!

MYRRHINE
　　　　　　　　I'm leaving.

CINESIAS
　Hold on! You might want to hear our child.
　Can you call out something to your mama?

CHILD
　Mummy, mummy, mummy!

CINESIAS
　　　　　　What's wrong with you?　　　　　[880]
　Don't you feel sorry for the boy. It's now
　six days since he's been washed or had some food.

MYRRHINE
　Ah yes, I pity him. But it's quite clear
　his father doesn't.

CINESIAS
　　　　　　　My lovely wife,
　come down here to the child.

MYRRHINE
　　　　　　　Being a mother
　is so demanding. I better go down.
　What I put up with!

[Myrrhine starts coming down from the Acropolis accentuating the movement of her hips as she goes]

CINESIAS
　　　　　　She seems to me
　to be much younger, easier on the eyes.
　She was acting like a shrew and haughty,
　but that just roused my passion even more.

MYRRHINE *[to the child]*
　My dear sweet little boy. But your father—
　such rotten one. Come here. I'll hold you.　　　[890]
　Mummy's little favourite.

ΚΙΝΗΣΙΑΣ

τί ὦ πονήρα ταῦτα ποιεῖς χἀτέραις
πείθει γυναιξί, κἀμέ τ' ἄχθεσθαι ποιεῖς
αὐτή τε λυπεῖ;

ΜΥΡΡΙΝΗ

μὴ πρόσαγε τὴν χεῖρά μοι.

ΚΙΝΗΣΙΑΣ

τὰ δ' ἔνδον ὄντα τἀμὰ καὶ σὰ χρήματα
χεῖρον διατίθης.   895

ΜΥΡΡΙΝΗ

ὀλίγον αὐτῶν μοι μέλει.

ΚΙΝΗΣΙΑΣ

ὀλίγον μέλει σοι τῆς κρόκης φορουμένης
ὑπὸ τῶν ἀλεκτρυόνων;

ΜΥΡΡΙΝΗ

ἔμοιγε νὴ Δία.

ΚΙΝΗΣΙΑΣ

τὰ ⟨δὲ⟩ τῆς Ἀφροδίτης ἱέρ' ἀνοργίαστά σοι
χρόνον τοσοῦτόν ἐστιν. οὐ βαδιεῖ πάλιν;

ΜΥΡΡΙΝΗ

μὰ Δί' οὐκ ἔγωγ', ἢν μὴ διαλλαχθῆτέ γε   900
καὶ τοῦ πολέμου παύσησθε.

ΚΙΝΗΣΙΑΣ

τοιγάρ, ἢν δοκῇ,
ποιήσομεν καὶ ταῦτα.

ΜΥΡΡΙΝΗ

τοιγάρ, ἢν δοκῇ,
κἀγώγ' ἄπειμ' ἐκεῖσε· νῦν δ' ἀπομώμοκα.

ΚΙΝΗΣΙΑΣ

σὺ δ' ἀλλὰ κατακλίνηθι μετ' ἐμοῦ διὰ χρόνου.

CINESIAS
                        You dim-witted girl,
    what are you doing, letting yourself
    be led on by these other women,
    causing me grief and injuring yourself?

MYRRHINE
    Don't lay a hand on me!

CINESIAS
                            Inside our home
    things are a mess. You stopped doing anything.

MYRRHINE
    I don't care.

CINESIAS
                    You don't care your weaving
    is being picked apart by hens?

MYRRHINE
                            So what?

CINESIAS
    You haven't honoured holy Aphrodite
    by having sex, not for a long time now.
    So won't you come back?

MYRRHINE
                        No, by god, I won't—   [900]
    unless you give me something in return.
    End this war.

CINESIAS
                    Well now, that's something I'll do,
    when it seems all right.

MYRRHINE
                        Well then, I'll leave here,
    when it seems all right. But now I'm under oath.

CINESIAS
    At least lie down with me a little while.

ΜΥΡΡΙΝΗ
  οὐ δῆτα· καίτοι σ᾽ οὐκ ἐρῶ γ᾽ ὡς οὐ φιλῶ.   905

ΚΙΝΗΣΙΑΣ
  φιλεῖς; τί οὖν οὐ κατεκλίνης ὦ Μύριον;

ΜΥΡΡΙΝΗ
  ὦ καταγέλαστ᾽ ἐναντίον τοῦ παιδίου;

ΚΙΝΗΣΙΑΣ
  μὰ Δί᾽ ἀλλὰ τοῦτό γ᾽ οἴκαδ᾽ ὦ Μανῆ φέρε.
  ἰδοὺ τὸ μέν σοι παιδίον καὶ δὴ 'κποδών,
  σὺ δ᾽ οὐ κατακλίνει.

ΜΥΡΡΙΝΗ
                        ποῦ γὰρ ἄν τις καὶ τάλαν   910
  δράσειε τοῦθ᾽;

ΚΙΝΗΣΙΑΣ
                  ὅπου; τὸ τοῦ Πανὸς καλόν.

ΜΥΡΡΙΝΗ
  καὶ πῶς ἔθ᾽ ἁγνὴ δῆτ᾽ ἂν ἔλθοιμ᾽ ἐς πόλιν;

ΚΙΝΗΣΙΑΣ
  κάλλιστα δήπου λουσαμένη τῇ Κλεψύδρᾳ.

ΜΥΡΡΙΝΗ
  ἔπειτ᾽ ὀμόσασα δῆτ᾽ ἐπιορκήσω τάλαν;

ΚΙΝΗΣΙΑΣ
  εἰς ἐμὲ τράποιτο· μηδὲν ὅρκου φροντίσῃς.   915

ΜΥΡΡΙΝΗ
  φέρε νυν ἐνέγκω κλινίδιον νῷν.

ΚΙΝΗΣΙΑΣ
                                  μηδαμῶς.
  ἀρκεῖ χαμαὶ νῷν.

MYRRHINE
    I can't. I'm not saying I wouldn't like to.

CINESIAS
    You'd like to? Then, my little Myrrhine,
    lie down right here.

MYRRHINE
                You must be joking—
    in front of our dear baby child?

CINESIAS
                   No, by god.

[Cinesias turns toward the attendant]

    Manes, take the boy back home. All right then,
    the lad's no longer in the way. Lie down.

MYRRHINE
    But, you silly man, where do we do it?   [910]

CINESIAS
    Where? The Cave of Pan's an excellent place.

MYRRHINE
    How will I purify myself when I return
    into the citadel?

CINESIAS
                You can wash yourself
    in the water clock. That would do the job.

MYRRHINE
    What about the oath I swore? Should I become
    a wretched perjurer?

CINESIAS
              I'll deal with that.
    Don't worry about the oath.

MYRRHINE
                  Well then,
    I'll go and get a bed for us.

CINESIAS
                No, no.
    The ground will do.

ΜΥΡΡΙΝΗ

μὰ τὸν Ἀπόλλω μή σ' ἐγὼ
καίπερ τοιοῦτον ὄντα κατακλινῶ χαμαί.

ΚΙΝΗΣΙΑΣ

ἦ τοι γυνὴ φιλεῖ με, δήλη 'στὶν καλῶς.

ΜΥΡΡΙΝΗ

ἰδοὺ κατάκεισ' ἀνύσας τι, κἀγὼ 'κδύομαι.   920
καίτοι, τὸ δεῖνα, ψίαθός ἐστ' ἐξοιστέα.

ΚΙΝΗΣΙΑΣ

ποία ψίαθος; μὴ μοί γε.

ΜΥΡΡΙΝΗ

νὴ τὴν Ἄρτεμιν,
αἰσχρὸν γὰρ ἐπὶ τόνου γε.

ΚΙΝΗΣΙΑΣ

δός μοί νυν κύσαι.

ΜΥΡΡΙΝΗ

ἰδού.

ΚΙΝΗΣΙΑΣ

παπαιάξ· ἧκέ νυν ταχέως πάνυ.

ΜΥΡΡΙΝΗ

ἰδοὺ ψίαθος· κατάκεισο, καὶ δὴ 'κδύομαι.   925
καίτοι, τὸ δεῖνα, προσκεφάλαιον οὐκ ἔχεις.

ΚΙΝΗΣΙΑΣ

ἀλλ' οὐδὲ δέομ' ἔγωγε.

MYRRHINE

                           No, by Apollo, no!
  You may be a rascal, but on the ground?
  No, I won't make you lie down there.

[Myrrhine goes back into the Acropolis to fetch a bed]

CINESIAS

                            Ah, my wife—
  she really loves me. That's so obvious.

[Myrrhine reappears carrying a small bed]

MYRRHINE

  Here we are. Get on there while I undress.   [920]
  O dear! I forgot to bring the mattress.

CINESIAS

  Why a mattress? I don't need that.

MYRRHINE

                       You can't lie
  on the bed cord. No, no, by Artemis,
  that would be a great disgrace.

CINESIAS

                    Give me a kiss—
  right now!

MYRRHINE *[kissing him]*

                There you go.

[Myrrhine goes back to the Acropolis to fetch the mattress]

CINESIAS

                  Oh my god—
  get back here quickly!

[Myrrhine reappears with the mattress]

MYRRHINE

                  Here's the mattress.
  You lie down on it. I'll get my clothes off.
  O dear me! You don't have a pillow.

CINESIAS

  But I don't need a pillow!

ΜΥΡΡΙΝΗ

νὴ Δί᾽ ἀλλ᾽ ἐγώ.

ΚΙΝΗΣΙΑΣ

ἀλλ᾽ ἢ τὸ πέος τόδ᾽ Ἡρακλῆς ξενίζεται.

ΜΥΡΡΙΝΗ

ἀνίστασ᾽, ἀναπήδησον. ἤδη πάντ᾽ ἔχω.

ΚΙΝΗΣΙΑΣ

ἅπαντα δῆτα. δεῦρό νυν ὦ χρύσιον.   930

ΜΥΡΡΙΝΗ

τὸ στρόφιον ἤδη λύομαι. μέμνησό νυν·
μή μ᾽ ἐξαπατήσῃς τὰ περὶ τῶν διαλλαγῶν.

ΚΙΝΗΣΙΑΣ

νὴ Δί᾽ ἀπολοίμην ἄρα.

ΜΥΡΡΙΝΗ

σισύραν οὐκ ἔχεις.

ΚΙΝΗΣΙΑΣ

μὰ Δί᾽ οὐδὲ δέομαί γ᾽, ἀλλὰ βινεῖν βούλομαι.

ΜΥΡΡΙΝΗ

ἀμέλει ποιήσεις τοῦτο· ταχὺ γὰρ ἔρχομαι.   935

ΚΙΝΗΣΙΑΣ

ἄνθρωπος ἐπιτρίψει με διὰ τὰ στρώματα.

ΜΥΡΡΙΝΗ

ἔπαιρε σαυτόν.

MYRRHINE

By god, I do.

[Myrrhine goes back to the Acropolis for a pillow]

CINESIAS

This cock of mine is just like Hercules—
he's being denied his supper.[45]

[Myrrhine returns with a pillow]

MYRRHINE

Lift up a bit.
Come on, up! There, I think that's everything.

CINESIAS

That's all we need. Come here, my treasure. [930]

MYRRHINE

I'm taking off the cloth around my breasts.
Now, don't forget. Don't you go lying to me
about that vote for peace.

CINESIAS

O my god,
may I die before that happens!

MYRRHINE

There's no blanket.

CINESIAS

I don't need one, by god! I want to get laid!

MYRRHINE

Don't worry. You will be. I'll be right back.

[Myrrhine goes back to the Acropolis to fetch a blanket]

CINESIAS

That woman's killing me with all the bedding!

[Myrrhine returns with a blanket]

MYRRHINE

All right, get up.

ΚΙΝΗΣΙΑΣ

ἀλλ᾽ ἐπῆρται τοῦτό γε.

ΜΥΡΡΙΝΗ

βούλει μυρίσω σε;

ΚΙΝΗΣΙΑΣ

μὰ τὸν Ἀπόλλω μὴ μέ γε.

ΜΥΡΡΙΝΗ

νὴ τὴν Ἀφροδίτην ἤν τε βούλῃ γ᾽ ἤν τε μή.

ΚΙΝΗΣΙΑΣ

εἶθ᾽ ἐκχυθείη τὸ μύρον ὦ Ζεῦ δέσποτα.   940

ΜΥΡΡΙΝΗ

πρότεινέ νυν τὴν χεῖρα κἀλείφου λαβών.

ΚΙΝΗΣΙΑΣ

οὐχ ἡδὺ τὸ μύρον μὰ τὸν Ἀπόλλω τουτογί,
εἰ μὴ διατριπτικόν γε κοὐκ ὄζον γάμων.

ΜΥΡΡΙΝΗ

τάλαιν᾽ ἐγὼ τὸ Ῥόδιον ἤνεγκον μύρον.

ΚΙΝΗΣΙΑΣ

ἀγαθόν· ἔα αὔτ᾽ ὦ δαιμονία.

ΜΥΡΡΙΝΗ

ληρεῖς ἔχων.   945

ΚΙΝΗΣΙΑΣ

κάκιστ᾽ ἀπόλοιθ᾽ ὁ πρῶτος ἑψήσας μύρον.

CINESIAS
                          But it's already up!

MYRRHINE
    You want me to rub some scent on you?

CINESIAS
    No, by Apollo. Not for me.

MYRRHINE
                          I'll do it,
    whether you want it rubbed on there or not—
    for Aphrodite's sake.

[Myrrhine goes back to the Acropolis to get the perfume]

CINESIAS
                    O great lord Zeus,   [940]
    pour the perfume out!

[Myrrhine returns with the perfume]

MYRRHINE
                    Hold out your hand, now.
    Take that and spread it round.

CINESIAS *[rubbing the perfume on himself]*
                          By Apollo,
    this stuff doesn't smell so sweet, not unless
    it's rubbed on thoroughly—no sexy smell.

MYRRHINE *[inspecting the jar of perfume]*
    I'm such a fool. I brought the Rhodian scent!

CINESIAS
    It's fine. Just let it go, my darling.

MYRRHINE *[getting up to leave]*
                          You're just saying that.

[Myrrhine goes back to the Acropolis to get the right perfume]

CINESIAS
    Damn the wretch who first came up with perfume!

ΜΥΡΡΙΝΗ
  λαβὲ τόνδε τὸν ἀλάβαστον.

ΚΙΝΗΣΙΑΣ
                                 ἀλλ᾽ ἕτερον ἔχω.
  ἀλλ᾽ ὠζυρὰ κατάκεισο καὶ μή μοι φέρε
  μηδέν.

ΜΥΡΡΙΝΗ
    ποιήσω ταῦτα νὴ τὴν Ἄρτεμιν.
  ὑπολύομαι γοῦν. ἀλλ᾽ ὅπως ὦ φίλτατε   950
  σπονδὰς ποιεῖσθαι ψηφιεῖ.

ΚΙΝΗΣΙΑΣ
                                 βουλεύσομαι.
  ἀπολώλεκέν με κἀπιτέτριφεν ἡ γυνὴ
  τά τ᾽ ἄλλα πάντα κἀποδείρασ᾽ οἴχεται.

ΚΙΝΗΣΙΑΣ
    οἴμοι τί πάθω; τίνα βινήσω
  τῆς καλλίστης πασῶν ψευσθείς;   955
  πῶς ταυτηνὶ παιδοτροφήσω;
      ποῦ Κυναλώπηξ;
      μίσθωσόν μοι τὴν τίτθην.

ΧΟΡΟΣ ΓΕΡΟΝΤΩΝ
    ἐν δεινῷ γ᾽ ὦ δύστηνε κακῷ
  τείρει ψυχὴν ἐξαπατηθείς.   960
  κἄγωγ᾽ οἰκτίρω σ᾽ αἰαῖ.
  ποῖος γὰρ ἂν ἢ νέφρος ἀντίσχοι,
  ποία ψυχή, ποῖοι δ᾽ ὄρχεις,
  ποία δ᾽ ὀσφῦς, ποῖος δ᾽ ὄρος
      κατατεινόμενος   965
      καὶ μὴ βινῶν τοὺς ὄρθρους;

ΚΙΝΗΣΙΑΣ
    ὦ Ζεῦ δεινῶν ἀντισπασμῶν.

[Myrrhine comes back from the Acropolis with another box of perfume]

MYRRHINE
> Grab this alabaster thing.

CINESIAS *[waving his cock]*
>> You grab this alabaster cock.
> Come lie down here, you tease. Don't go and fetch
> another thing for me.

MYRRHINE
>> By Artemis, I'll grab it.
> I'm taking off my shoes. Now, my darling,   [950]
> you will be voting to bring on a peace.

CINESIAS
> I'm planning to.

[Myrrhine goes back to the Acropolis. Cinesias turns and sees she's gone]

>> That woman's killing me!
> She teased me, got me all inflamed, then left.

[Cinesias gets up and declaims in a parody of tragic style]

Alas, why suffer from such agony?
> Who can I screw? Why'd she betray me,
> the most beautiful woman of them all?
> Poor little cock, how can I care for you?
> Where's that Cynalopex? I'll pay him well
> to nurse this little fellow back to health.[16]

LEADER OF MEN'S CHORUS
> You poor man, in such a fix—your spirit
> so tricked and in distress. I pity you.   [960]
> How can your kidneys stand the strain,
> your balls, your loins, your bum, your brain
> endure an erection that's hard for you,
> without a chance of a morning screw.

CINESIAS
> O mighty Zeus, it's started throbbing once again.

ΧΟΡΟΣ ΓΕΡΟΝΤΩΝ
ταυτὶ μέντοι νυνί σ' ἐποίησ'
ἡ παμβδελυρὰ καὶ παμμυσαρά.

ΚΙΝΗΣΙΑΣ
μὰ Δί' ἀλλὰ φίλη καὶ παγγλυκερά.   970

ΧΟΡΟΣ ΓΕΡΟΝΤΩΝ
ποία γλυκερά; μιαρὰ μιαρά.

ΚΙΝΗΣΙΑΣ
⟨μιαρὰ⟩ δῆτ' ὦ Ζεῦ ὦ Ζεῦ·
εἴθ' αὐτὴν ὥσπερ τοὺς θωμοὺς
μεγάλῳ τυφῷ καὶ πρηστῆρι
ξυστρέψας καὶ ξυγγογγύλας   975
οἴχοιο φέρων, εἶτα μεθείης,
ἡ δὲ φέροιτ' αὖ πάλιν ἐς τὴν γῆν,
κᾆτ' ἐξαίφνης
περὶ τὴν ψωλὴν περιβαίη.

ΚΗΡΥΞ ΛΑΚΕΔΑΙΜΟΝΙΩΝ
πᾷ τᾶν Ἀσανᾶν ἐστιν ἁ γερωχία   980
ἢ τοὶ πρυτάνιες; λῶ τι μυσίξαι νέον.

ΚΙΝΗΣΙΑΣ
σὺ δ' εἶ πότερον ἄνθρωπος ἢ κονίσαλος;

ΚΗΡΥΞ ΛΑΚΕΔΑΙΜΟΝΙΩΝ
κᾶρυξ ἐγὼν ὦ κυρσάνιε ναὶ τὼ σιὼ
ἔμολον ἀπὸ Σπάρτας περὶ τᾶν διαλλαγᾶν.

ΚΙΝΗΣΙΑΣ
κἄπειτα δόρυ δῆθ' ὑπὸ μάλης ἥκεις ἔχων;   985

ΚΗΡΥΞ ΛΑΚΕΔΑΙΜΟΝΙΩΝ
οὐ τὸν Δί' οὐκ ἐγών γα.

LEADER OF MEN'S CHORUS
    A dirty stinking bitch did this to you.

CINESIAS
    No, by god, a loving girl, a sweet one, too.   [970]

LEADER OF MEN'S CHORUS
    Sweet? Not her. She's a tease, a slut.

CINESIAS
    All right, she is a tease, but—
    O Zeus, Zeus, I wish
    you'd sweep her up there
    in a great driving storm,
    like dust in the air,
    whirl her around,
    then fall to the ground.
    And as she's carried down,
    to earth one more time,
    let her fall right away
    on this pecker of mine.

[Enter the Spartan herald. He, too, has a giant erection, which he is trying to hide under his cloak]

SPARTAN HERALD
    Where's the Athenian Senate and the Prytanes?[47]   [980]
    I come with fresh dispatches.

CINESIAS *[looking at the Herald's erection]*
                            Are you a man,
    or some phallic monster?

SPARTAN HERALD
                            I'm a herald,
    by the twin gods. And my good man,
    I come from Sparta with a proposal,
    arrangements for a truce.

CINESIAS
                            If that's the case,
    why do you have a spear concealed in there?

SPARTAN HERALD
    I'm not concealing anything, by god.

115

ΚΙΝΗΣΙΑΣ

ποῖ μεταστρέφει;
τί δὴ προβάλλει τὴν χλαμύδ᾽; ἢ βουβωνιᾷς
ὑπὸ τῆς ὁδοῦ;

ΚΗΡΥΞ ΛΑΚΕΔΑΙΜΟΝΙΩΝ

παλαιόρ γα ναὶ τὸν Κάστορα
ὤνθρωπος.

ΚΙΝΗΣΙΑΣ

ἀλλ᾽ ἔστυκας ὦ μιαρώτατε.

ΚΗΡΥΞ ΛΑΚΕΔΑΙΜΟΝΙΩΝ

οὐ τὸν Δί᾽ οὐκ ἐγών γα· μηδ᾽ αὖ πλαδδίη.   990

ΚΙΝΗΣΙΑΣ

τί δ᾽ ἐστί σοι τοδί;

ΚΗΡΥΞ ΛΑΚΕΔΑΙΜΟΝΙΩΝ

σκυτάλα Λακωνικά.

ΚΙΝΗΣΙΑΣ

εἴπερ γε χαὔτη 'στὶ σκυτάλη Λακωνική.
ἀλλ᾽ ὡς πρὸς εἰδότ᾽ ἐμὲ σὺ τἀληθῆ λέγε.
τί τὰ πράγμαθ᾽ ὑμῖν ἐστι τὰν Λακεδαίμονι;

ΚΗΡΥΞ ΛΑΚΕΔΑΙΜΟΝΙΩΝ

ὀρσὰ Λακεδαίμων πᾶα καὶ τοὶ σύμμαχοι   995
ἄπαντες ἐστύκαντι· Πελλάνας δὲ δεῖ.

ΚΙΝΗΣΙΑΣ

ἀπὸ τοῦ δὲ τουτὶ τὸ κακὸν ὑμῖν ἐνέπεσεν;
ἀπὸ Πανός;

ΚΗΡΥΞ ΛΑΚΕΔΑΙΜΟΝΙΩΝ

οὔκ, ἀλλ᾽ ἆρχεν οἰῶ Λαμπιτώ,
ἔπειτα τἆλλαι ταὶ κατὰ Σπάρταν ἅμα
γυναῖκες περ ἀπὸ μιᾶς ὑσπλαγίδος   1000
ἀπήλααν τὼς ἄνδρας ἀπὸ τῶν ὑσσάκων.

CINESIAS
>Then why are you turning to one side?
>What that thing there, sticking from your cloak?
>Has your journey made your groin inflamed?

SPARTAN HERALD
>By old Castor, this man's insane!

CINESIAS
>   You rogue,
>   you've got a hard on!

SPARTAN HERALD
>   No I don't, I tell you.   [990]
>   Let's have no more nonsense.

CINESIAS [*pointing to the herald's erection*]
>   Then what's that?

SPARTAN HERALD
>   It's a Spartan herald's stick.

CINESIAS
>   O that's what it is,
>   a Spartan herald stick. Let's have a chat.
>   Tell me the truth. How are things going for you
>   out there in Sparta?

SPARTAN HERALD
>   Not good. The Spartans
>   are all standing tall and the allies, too—
>   everyone is firm and hard. We need a thrust
>   in someone's rear.[48]

CINESIAS
>   This trouble of yours—
>   where did it come from? Was it from Pan?[49]

SPARTAN HERALD
>   No. I think it started with Lampito.
>   Then, at her suggestion, other women
>   in Sparta, as if from one starting gate,
>   ran off to keep men from their honey pots.[50]   [1000]

117

ΚΙΝΗΣΙΑΣ

πῶς οὖν ἔχετε;

ΚΗΡΥΞ ΛΑΚΕΔΑΙΜΟΝΙΩΝ

μογίομες. ἂν γὰρ τὰν πόλιν
ᾇπερ λυχνοφορίοντες ἐπικεκύφαμες.
ταὶ γὰρ γυναῖκες οὐδὲ τῶ μύρτω σιγεῖν
ἐῶντι, πρίν γ' ἅπαντες ἐξ ἑνὸς λόγω   1005
σπονδὰς ποιησώμεσθα ποττὰν Ἑλλάδα.

ΚΙΝΗΣΙΑΣ

τουτὶ τὸ πρᾶγμα πανταχόθεν ξυνομώμοται
ὑπὸ τῶν γυναικῶν· ἄρτι νυνὶ μανθάνω.
ἀλλ' ὡς τάχιστα φράζε περὶ διαλλαγῶν
αὐτοκράτορας πρέσβεις ἀποπέμπειν ἐνθαδί.   1010
ἐγὼ δ' ἑτέρους ἐνθένδε τῇ βουλῇ φράσω
πρέσβεις ἑλέσθαι τὸ πέος ἐπιδείξας τοδί.

ΚΗΡΥΞ ΛΑΚΕΔΑΙΜΟΝΙΩΝ

ποτάομαι· κράτιστα γὰρ παντᾷ λέγεις.

ΧΟΡΟΣ ΓΕΡΟΝΤΩΝ

οὐδέν ἐστι θηρίον γυναικὸς ἀμαχώτερον,
οὐδὲ πῦρ, οὐδ' ὧδ' ἀναιδὴς οὐδεμία πόρδαλις.   1015

ΧΟΡΟΣ ΓΥΝΑΙΚΩΝ

ταῦτα μέντοι <σὺ> ξυνιεὶς εἶτα πολεμεῖς ἐμοί,
ἐξὸν ὦ πόνηρε σοὶ βέβαιον ἔμ' ἔχειν φίλην;

ΧΟΡΟΣ ΓΕΡΟΝΤΩΝ

ὡς ἐγὼ μισῶν γυναῖκας οὐδέποτε παύσομαι.

ΧΟΡΟΣ ΓΥΝΑΙΚΩΝ

ἀλλ' ὅταν βούλῃ σύ· νῦν δ' οὖν οὔ σε περιόψομαι
γυμνὸν ὄνθ' οὕτως. ὁρῶ γὰρ ὡς καταγέλαστος εἶ.   1020
ἀλλὰ τὴν ἐξωμίδ' ἐνδύσω σε προσιοῦσ' ἐγώ.

CINESIAS
How are you doing?

SPARTAN HERALD
                    We're all in pain.
We go around the city doubled up,
like men who light the lamps.[51] The women
won't let us touch their pussies, not until
we've made a peace with all of Greece.

CINESIAS
                                This matter
is a female plot, a grand conspiracy
affecting all of Greece. Now I understand.
Return to Sparta as fast as you can go.
Tell them they must send out ambassadors   [1010]
with full authority to deal for peace.
I'll tell our leaders here to make a choice
of our ambassadors. I'll show them my prick.

SPARTAN HERALD
All you've said is good advice. I must fly.

[Cinesias and the Spartan Herald exit in opposite directions]

LEADER OF MEN'S CHORUS
There's no wild animal harder to control
than women, not even blazing fire.
The panther itself displays more shame.

LEADER OF WOMEN'S CHORUS
If you know that, then why wage war with me?
You old scoundrel, we could be lasting friends.

LEADER OF MEN'S CHORUS
But my hatred for women will not stop!

LEADER OF WOMEN'S CHORUS
Whatever you want. But I don't much like
to look at you like this, without your clothes.   [1020]
It makes me realize how silly you are.
Look, I'll come over and put your shirt on.

*[The Leader of the Women's Chorus picks up a tunic, goes over to the
Leader of the Men's Chorus, and helps him put it on.]*

Aristophanes

ΧΟΡΟΣ ΓΕΡΟΝΤΩΝ

τοῦτο μὲν μὰ τὸν Δί᾿ οὐ πονηρὸν ἐποιήσατε·
ἀλλ᾿ ὑπ᾿ ὀργῆς γὰρ πονηρᾶς καὶ τότ᾿ ἀπέδυν ἐγώ.

ΧΟΡΟΣ ΓΥΝΑΙΚΩΝ

πρῶτα μὲν φαίνει γ᾿ ἀνήρ, εἶτ᾿ οὐ καταγέλαστος εἶ.
κεἴ με μὴ ᾿λύπεις, ἐγώ σου κἂν τόδε τὸ θηρίον   1025
τοὐπὶ τὠφθαλμῷ λαβοῦσ᾿ ἐξεῖλον ἂν ὃ νῦν ἔνι.

ΧΟΡΟΣ ΓΕΡΟΝΤΩΝ

τοῦτ᾿ ἄρ᾿ ἦν με τοὐπιτρῖβον, δακτύλιος οὑτοσί·
ἐκσκάλευσον αὐτό, κᾆτα δεῖξον ἀφελοῦσά μοι·
ὡς τὸν ὀφθαλμόν γέ μου νὴ τὸν Δία πάλαι δάκνει.

ΧΟΡΟΣ ΓΥΝΑΙΚΩΝ

ἀλλὰ δράσω ταῦτα· καίτοι δύσκολος ἔφυς ἀνήρ.   1030
ἦ μέγ᾿ ὦ Ζεῦ χρῆμ᾿ ἰδεῖν τῆς ἐμπίδος ἔνεστί σοι.
οὐχ ὁρᾷς; οὐκ ἐμπίς ἐστιν ἥδε Τρικορυσία;

ΧΟΡΟΣ ΓΕΡΟΝΤΩΝ

νὴ Δί᾿ ὤνησάς γέ μ᾿, ὡς πάλαι γέ μ᾿ ἐφρεωρύχει,
ὥστ᾿ ἐπειδὴ ᾿ξῃρέθη, ῥεῖ μου τὸ δάκρυον πολύ.

ΧΟΡΟΣ ΓΥΝΑΙΚΩΝ

ἀλλ᾿ ἀποψήσω σ᾿ ἐγώ, καίτοι πάνυ πονηρὸς εἶ,   1035
καὶ φιλήσω.

ΧΟΡΟΣ ΓΕΡΟΝΤΩΝ

          μὴ φιλήσῃς.

ΧΟΡΟΣ ΓΥΝΑΙΚΩΝ

                    ἤν τε βούλῃ γ᾿ ἤν τε μή.

ΧΟΡΟΣ ΓΕΡΟΝΤΩΝ

ἀλλὰ μὴ ὥρασ᾿ ἵκοισθ᾿· ὡς ἐστὲ θωπικαὶ φύσει,
κᾆστ᾿ ἐκεῖνο τοὔπος ὀρθῶς κοὐ κακῶς εἰρημένον,
οὔτε σὺν πανωλέθροισιν οὔτ᾿ ἄνευ πανωλέθρων.

LEADER OF MEN'S CHORUS
  By god, what you've just done is not so bad.
  I took it off in a fit of stupid rage.

LEADER OF WOMEN'S CHORUS
  Now at least you look like a man again.
  And people won't find you ridiculous.
  If you hadn't been so nasty to me,
  I'd grab that insect stuck in your eye
  and pull it out. It's still in there.

LEADER OF MEN'S CHORUS
  So that's what's been troubling me. Here's a ring.
  Scrape it off. Get it out and show it to me.
  God, that's been bothering my eye for ages.

[The Leader of the Women's Chorus takes the ring and inspects the Leader of the Men's Chorus in the eye]

LEADER OF WOMEN'S CHORUS
  I'll do it. You men are born hard to please.   [1030]
  My god, you picked up a monstrous insect.
  Have a look. That's a Tricorynthus bug!⁵²

LEADER OF MEN'S CHORUS
  By Zeus, you've been a mighty help to me.
  That thing's been digging wells in me a while.
  Now it's been removed, my eyes are streaming.

LEADER OF WOMEN'S CHORUS
  I'll wipe it for you, though you're a scoundrel.
  I'll give you a kiss.

LEADER OF MEN'S CHORUS
                        I don't want a kiss.

LEADER OF WOMEN'S CHORUS
  I'll will, whether it's what you want or not.

[She kisses him]

LEADER OF MEN'S CHORUS
  O you've got me. You're born to flatter us.
  That saying got it right—it states the case
  quite well, "These women—one has no life
  with them, and cannot live without them."

Aristophanes

ἀλλὰ νυνὶ σπένδομαί σοι, καὶ τὸ λοιπὸν οὐκέτι 1040
οὔτε δράσω φλαῦρον οὐδὲν οὔθ' ὑφ' ὑμῶν πείσομαι.
ἀλλὰ κοινῇ συσταλέντες τοῦ μέλους ἀρξώμεθα.

ΧΟΡΟΣ
    οὐ παρασκευαζόμεσθα
    τῶν πολιτῶν οὐδέν' ὦνδρες
    φλαῦρον εἰπεῖν οὐδὲ ἕν. 1045
ἀλλὰ πολὺ τοὔμπαλιν πάντ' ἀγαθὰ καὶ λέγειν
καὶ δρᾶν· ἱκανὰ γὰρ τὰ κακὰ καὶ τὰ παρακείμενα.
ἀλλ' ἐπαγγελλέτω πᾶς ἀνὴρ καὶ γυνή,
    εἴ τις ἀργυρίδιον δεῖται 1050
    λαβεῖν μνᾶς ἢ δύ' ἢ τρεῖς,
      ὡς πόλλ' ἔσω 'στὶν
    κἄχομεν βαλλάντια.
    κἄν ποτ' εἰρήνη φανῇ,
    ὅστις ἂν νυνὶ δανείση- 1055
      ται παρ' ἡμῶν,
    ἂν λάβῃ μηκέτ' ἀποδῷ.

    ἑστιᾶν δὲ μέλλομεν ξέ-
    νους τινὰς Καρυστίους, ἄν-
    δρας καλούς τε κἀγαθούς. 1060
κἄστιν ⟨ἔτ'⟩ ἔτνος τι· καὶ δελφάκιον ἦν τί μοι,
καὶ τοῦτο τέθυχ', ὡς τὰ κρέ' ἔδεσθ' ἁπαλὰ καὶ καλά.
ἥκετ' οὖν εἰς ἐμοῦ τήμερον· πρῲ δὲ χρὴ
    τοῦτο δρᾶν λελουμένους αὔ-
    τούς τε καὶ τὰ παιδί', εἶτ' εἴ-
      σω βαδίζειν, 1065
    μηδ' ἐρέσθαι μηδένα,
    ἀλλὰ χωρεῖν ἄντικρυς
    ὥσπερ οἴκαδ' εἰς ἑαυτῶν
      γεννικῶς, ὡς 1070
    ἡ θύρα κεκλήσεται.

— καὶ μὴν ἀπὸ τῆς Σπάρτης οἰδὶ πρέσβεις ἕλκοντες ὑπήνας
χωροῦσ', ὥσπερ χοιροκομεῖον περὶ τοῖς μηροῖσιν ἔχοντες.

But now I'll make a truce with you. I won't   [1040]
insult you any more in days to come,
and you won't make me suffer. So now,
let's make a common group and sing a song.

[The Men's and Women's Choruses combine]

COMBINED CHORUS *[addressing the audience]*
    You citizens, we're not inclined
    with any of you to be unkind.
    Just the reverse—our words to you
    will be quite nice. We'll act well, too.
    For now we've had enough bad news.
    So if a man or woman here   [1050]
    needs ready cash, give out a cheer,
    and take some minae, two or three.
    Coins fill our purses now, you see.
    And if we get a peace treaty,
    you take some money from the sack,
    and keep it. You don't pay it back.

    I'm going to have a great shindig—
    I've got some soup, I'll kill a pig—
    with friends of mine from Carystia.⁵³   [1060]
    You'll eat fine tender meat again.
    Come to my house this very day.
    But first wash all the dirt away,
    you and your kids, then walk on by.
    No need to ask a person why.
    Just come straight in, as if my home
    was like your own—for at my place   [1070]
    we'll shut the door right in your face.

[A group of Spartans enters]

LEADER OF THE CHORUS
    Ah, here come the Spartan ambassadors
    trailing their long beards. They've got
    something like a pig pen between their thighs.

*[The Spartan ambassadors enter, moving with difficulty because of their
enormous erections.]*

Aristophanes

ἄνδρες Λάκωνες πρῶτα μέν μοι χαίρετε,
εἶτ᾽ εἴπαθ᾽ ἡμῖν πῶς ἔχοντες ἥκετε.   1075

ΛΑΚΩΝ

τί δεῖ ποθ᾽ ὑμὲ πολλὰ μυσίδδειν ἔπη;
ὁρῆν γὰρ ἔξεσθ᾽ ὡς ἔχοντες ἵκομες.

ΧΟΡΟΣ

βαβαί· νενεύρωται μὲν ἥδε συμφορὰ
δεινῶς, τεθερμῶσθαί γε χεῖρον φαίνεται.

ΛΑΚΩΝ

ἄφατα. τί κα λέγοι τις; ἀλλ᾽ ὄπᾳ σέλει   1080
παντᾷ τις ἐλσὼν ἁμὶν εἰράναν σέτω.

ΧΟΡΟΣ

καὶ μὴν ὁρῶ καὶ τούσδε τοὺς αὐτόχθονας
ὥσπερ παλαιστὰς ἄνδρας ἀπὸ τῶν γαστέρων
θαἰμάτι᾽ ἀποστέλλοντας· ὥστε φαίνεται
ἀσκητικὸν τὸ χρῆμα τοῦ νοσήματος.   1085

ΑΘΗΝΑΙΟΣ

τίς ἂν φράσεις ποῦ᾽ στιν ἡ Λυσιστράτη;
ὡς ἄνδρες ἡμεῖς οὑτοιὶ τοιουτοί.

ΧΟΡΟΣ

χαὔτη ξυνᾴδει χἠτέρα ταύτῃ νόσῳ.
ἦ που πρὸς ὄρθρον σπασμὸς ὑμᾶς λαμβάνει;

ΑΘΗΝΑΙΟΣ

μὰ Δί᾽ ἀλλὰ ταυτὶ δρῶντες ἐπιτετρίμμεθα.   1090
ὥστ᾽ εἴ τις ἡμᾶς μὴ διαλλάξει ταχύ,
οὐκ ἔσθ᾽ ὅπως οὐ Κλεισθένη βινήσομεν.

ΧΟΡΟΣ

εἰ σωφρονεῖτε, θαἰμάτια λήψεσθ᾽, ὅπως
τῶν Ἑρμοκοπιδῶν μή τις ὑμᾶς ὄψεται.

124

Men of Sparta, first of all, our greetings.
Tell us how you are. Why have you come?

SPARTAN AMBASSADOR
Why waste a lot of words to tell you?
You see the state that brought us here.

[The Spartans all display their erections with military precision]

LEADER OF THE CHORUS
Oh my! The crisis has grown more severe.
It seems the strain is worse than ever.

SPARTAN AMBASSADOR
It's indescribable. What can I say? [1080]
But let someone come, give us a peace
in any way he can.

LEADER OF THE CHORUS
Well now, I see
our own ambassadors—they look just like
our wrestling men with their shirts sticking out
around their bellies or like athletic types
who need to exercise to cure their sickness.

ATHENIAN AMBASSADOR
Where's Lysistrata? Can someone tell me?
We're men here and, well, look . . .

*[The Athenians pull back their cloaks and reveal that, like the Spartans,
they all have giant erections]*

LEADER OF THE CHORUS
They're clearly suffering from the same disease.
Hey, does it throb early in the morning?

ATHENIAN AMBASSADOR
By god, yes. What this is doing to me— [1090]
it's torture. If we don't get a treaty soon
we'll going to have to cornhole Cleisthenes.54

LEADER OF THE CHORUS
If you're smart, keep it covered with your cloak.
One of those men who chopped off Hermes' dick
might see you.55

ΑΘΗΝΑΙΟΣ
νὴ τὸν Δί᾽ εὖ μέντοι λέγεις.

ΛΑΚΩΝ
ναὶ τὼ σιὼ   1095
παντᾷ γα. φέρε τὸ ἔσθος ἀμβαλώμεθα.

ΑΘΗΝΑΙΟΣ
ὦ χαίρετ᾽ ὦ Λάκωνες· αἰσχρά γ᾽ ἐπάθομεν.

ΛΑΚΩΝ
ὦ Πολυχαρείδα δεινά κ᾽ αὖ ᾽πεπόνθεμες,
αἰ εἶδον ἁμὲ τὦνδρες ἀμπεφλασμένως.

ΑΘΗΝΑΙΟΣ
ἄγε δὴ Λάκωνες αὖθ᾽ ἕκαστα χρὴ λέγειν.   1100
ἐπὶ τί πάρεστε δεῦρο;

ΛΑΚΩΝ
περὶ διαλλαγᾶν
πρέσβεις.

ΑΘΗΝΑΙΟΣ
καλῶς δὴ λέγετε· χἠμεῖς τουτογί.
τί οὐ καλοῦμεν δῆτα τὴν Λυσιστράην,
ἥπερ διαλλάξειεν ἡμᾶς ἂν μόνη;

ΛΑΚΩΝ
ναὶ τὼ σιὼ κἂν λῆτε τὸν Λυσίστρατον.   1105

ΑΘΗΝΑΙΟΣ
ἀλλ᾽ οὐδὲν ἡμᾶς, ὡς ἔοικε, δεῖ καλεῖν·
αὐτὴ γάρ, ὡς ἤκουσεν, ἥδ᾽ ἐξέρχεται.

ΧΟΡΟΣ
χαῖρ᾽ ὦ πασῶν ἀνδρειοτάτη· δεῖ δὴ νυνί σε γενέσθαι
δεινὴν ⟨δειλὴν⟩ ἀγαθὴν φαύλην σεμνὴν ἀγανὴν
πολύπειρον·
ὡς οἱ πρῶτοι τῶν Ἑλλήνων τῇ σῇ ληφθέντες ἴυγγι   1110
συνεχώρησάν σοι καὶ κοινῇ τἀγκλήματα πάντ᾽ ἐπέτρεψαν.

ATHENIAN AMBASSADOR *[pulling his cloak over his erection]*
        By god, that's good advice.

SPARTAN AMBASSADOR *[doing the same]*
    Yes, by the twin gods, excellent advice.
    I'll pull my mantle over it.

ATHENIAN AMBASSADOR
              Greetings, Spartans.
    We're both suffering disgracefully.

SPARTAN AMBASSADOR
    Yes, dear sir, we'd have been in real pain
    if one of those dick-clippers had seen us
    with our peckers sticking up like this.

ATHENIAN AMBASSADOR
    All right, Spartans, we each need to talk.   [1100]
    Why are you here?

SPARTAN AMBASSADOR
              Ambassadors for peace.

ATHENIAN AMBASSADOR
    Well said. We want the same. Why don't we call
    Lysistrata. She's the only one who'll bring
    a resolution to our differences.

SPARTAN AMBASSADOR
    By the two gods, bring in Lysistratus,
    if he's the ambassador you want.

[Lysistrata emerges from the gates of the citadel]

ATHENIAN AMBASSADOR
    It seems there is no need to summon her.
    She's heard us, and here she is in person.

LEADER OF THE CHORUS
    Hail to the bravest woman of them all.
    You must now show that you're resilient—
    stern but yielding, with a good heart but mean,
    stately but down-to-earth. The foremost men
    in all of Greece in deference to your charms   [1110]
    have come together here before you
    so you can arbitrate all their complaints.

ΛΥΣΙΣΤΡΑΤΗ

ἀλλ᾽ οὐχὶ χαλεπὸν τοὖργον, εἰ λάβοι γέ τις

ὀργῶντας ἀλλήλων τε μὴ ᾽κπειρωμένους.

τάχα δ᾽ εἴσομαι ᾽γώ. ποῦ ᾽στιν ἡ Διαλλαγή;

πρόσαγε λαβοῦσα πρῶτα τοὺς Λακωνικούς,   1115

καὶ μὴ χαλεπῇ τῇ χειρὶ μηδ᾽ αὐθαδικῇ,

μηδ᾽ ὥσπερ ἡμῶν ἄνδρες ἀμαθῶς τοῦτ᾽ ἔδρων,

ἀλλ᾽ ὡς γυναῖκας εἰκός, οἰκείως πάνυ,

ἢν μὴ διδῷ τὴν χεῖρα, τῆς σάθης ἄγε.

ἴθι καὶ σὺ τούτους τοὺς Ἀθηναίους ἄγε,   1120

οὗ δ᾽ ἂν διδῶσι πρόσαγε τούτους λαβομένη.

ἄνδρες Λάκωνες στῆτε παρ᾽ ἐμὲ πλησίον,

ἐνθένδε δ᾽ ὑμεῖς, καὶ λόγων ἀκούσατε.

ἐγὼ γυνὴ μέν εἰμι, νοῦς δ᾽ ἔνεστί μοι,

αὐτὴ δ᾽ ἐμαυτῆς οὐ κακῶς γνώμης ἔχω,   1125

τοὺς δ᾽ ἐκ πατρός τε καὶ γεραιτέρων λόγους

πολλοὺς ἀκούσασ᾽ οὐ μεμούσωμαι κακῶς.

λαβοῦσα δ᾽ ὑμᾶς λοιδορῆσαι βούλομαι

κοινῇ δικαίως, οἳ μιᾶς ἐκ χέρνιβος

βωμοὺς περιραίνοντες ὥσπερ ξυγγενεῖς   1130

Ὀλυμπίασιν, ἐν Πύλαις, Πυθοῖ (πόσους

εἴποιμ᾽ ἂν ἄλλους, εἴ με μηκύνειν δέοι;)

ἐχθρῶν παρόντων βαρβάρων στρατεύματι

Ἕλληνας ἄνδρας καὶ πόλεις ἀπόλλυτε.

εἷς μὲν λόγος μοι δεῦρ᾽ ἀεὶ περαίνεται.   1135

LYSISTRATA
   That task should not be difficult, unless
   they're so aroused they screw each other.
   I'll quickly notice that. But where is she,
   the young girl Reconciliation?

[The personification of the the goddess Reconciliation comes out. She's completely naked. Lysistrata addresses her first][56]

                    Come here,
   and first, take hold of those from Sparta,
   don't grab too hard or be too rough, not like
   our men who act so boorishly—instead
   do it as women do when they're at home.
   If they won't extend their hands to you,
   then grab their cocks.

[Reconciliation takes two Spartans by their penises and leads them over to Lysistrata]

                    Now go and do the same   [1120]
   for the Athenians. You can hold them
   by whatever they stick out.

[Reconciliation leads the Athenians over to Lysistrata]

                    Now then,
   you men of Sparta, stand here close to me,
   and you Athenians over here. All of you,
   listen to my words. I am a woman,
   but I have a brain, and my common sense
   is not so bad—I picked it up quite well
   from listening to my father and to speeches
   from our senior men. Now I've got you here,
   I wish to reprimand you, both of you,
   and rightly so. At Olympia, Delphi,   [1130]
   and Thermopylae (I could mention
   many other places if I had a mind
   to make it a long list) both of you
   use the same cup when you sprinkle altars,
   as if you share the same ancestral group.[57]
   We've got barbarian enemies, and yet
   with your armed expeditions you destroy
   Greek men and cities. At this point, I'll end
   the first part of my speech.

ΑΘΗΝΑΙΟΣ

    ἐγὼ δ᾽ ἀπόλλυμαί γ᾽ ἀπεψωλημένος.

ΛΥΣΙΣΤΡΑΤΗ

    εἶτ᾽ ὦ Λάκωνες, πρὸς γὰρ ὑμᾶς τρέψομαι,
    οὐκ ἴσθ᾽ ὅτ᾽ ἐλθὼν δεῦρο Περικλείδας ποτὲ
    ὁ Λάκων Ἀθηναίων ἱκέτης καθέζετο
    ἐπὶ τοῖσι βωμοῖς ὠχρὸς ἐν φοινικίδι   1140
    στρατιὰν προσαιτῶν; ἡ δὲ Μεσσήνη τότε
    ὑμῖν ἐπέκειτο χὠ θεὸς σείων ἅμα.
    ἐλθὼν δὲ σὺν ὁπλίταισι τετρακισχιλίοις
    Κίμων ὅλην ἔσωσε τὴν Λακεδαίμονα.
    ταυτὶ παθόντες τῶν Ἀθηναίων ὕπο   1145
    δῃοῦτε χώραν, ἧς ὑπ᾽ εὖ πεπόνθατε;

ΑΘΗΝΑΙΟΣ

    ἀδικοῦσιν οὗτοι νὴ Δί᾽ ὦ Λυσιστράτη.

ΛΑΚΩΝ

    ἀδικίομες· ἀλλ᾽ ὁ πρωκτὸς ἄφατον ὡς καλός.

ΛΥΣΙΣΤΡΑΤΗ

    ὑμᾶς δ᾽ ἀφήσειν τοὺς Ἀθηναίους <μ᾽> οἴει;
    οὐκ ἴσθ᾽ ὅθ᾽ ὑμᾶς οἱ Λάκωνες αὖθις αὖ   1150
    κατωνάκας φοροῦντας ἐλθόντες δορὶ
    πολλοὺς μὲν ἄνδρας Θετταλῶν ἀπώλεσαν,
    πολλοὺς δ᾽ ἑταίρους Ἱππίου καὶ ξυμμάχους,
    ξυνεκμαχοῦντες τῇ τόθ᾽ ἡμέρᾳ μόνοι,
    κἠλευθέρωσαν κἀντὶ τῆς κατωνάκης   1155
    τὸν δῆμον ὑμῶν χλαῖναν ἠμπέσχον πάλιν;

ΛΑΚΩΝ

    οὔπα γυναῖκ᾽ ὄπωπα χαϊωτέραν.

ΑΘΗΝΑΙΟΣ

    ἐγὼ δὲ κύσθον γ᾽ οὐδέπω καλλίονα.

ATHENIAN AMBASSADOR
                              This erection—
    it's killing me!

LYSISTRATA
                              And now you Spartans,
    I'll turn to you. Don't you remember how,
    some time ago, Periclidias came,
    a fellow Spartan, and sat down right here,
    a suppliant at these Athenian altars—   [1140]
    he looked so pale there in his purple robes—
    begging for an army? Messenians then
    were pressing you so hard, just at the time
    god sent the earthquake. So Cimon set out
    with four thousand armed infantry and saved
    the whole of Sparta.⁵⁸ After going through that,
    how can you ravage the Athenians' land,
    the ones who helped you out?

ATHENIAN AMBASSADOR
                              Lysistrata,
    you're right, by god. They're in the wrong.

SPARTAN AMBASSADOR *[looking at Reconciliation]*
                              Not true,
    but look at that incredibly fine ass!

LYSISTRATA
    Do you Athenians think I'll forget you?
    Don't you remember how these Spartans men,   [1150]
    back in the days when you were dressed as slaves
    came here with spears and totally destroyed
    those hordes from Thessaly and many friends
    of Hippias and those allied with him?
    It took them just one day to drive them out
    and set you free. At that point you exchanged
    your slavish clothes for cloaks which free men wear.

SPARTAN AMBASSADOR
    I've never seen a more gracious woman.

ATHENIAN AMBASSADOR *[looking at Reconciliation]*
    I've never seen a finer looking pussy.

ΛΥΣΙΣΤΡΑΤΗ

τί δῆθ᾽ ὑπηργμένων γε πολλῶν κἀγαθῶν
μάχεσθε κοὐ παύεσθε τῆς μοχθηρίας;
τί δ᾽ οὐ διηλλάγητε; φέρε τί τοὐμποδών;

1160

ΛΑΚΩΝ

ἀμές γε λῶμες, αἴ τις ἀμὶν τὦγκυκλον
λῇ τοῦτ᾽ ἀποδόμεν.

ΛΥΣΙΣΤΡΑΤΗ

ποῖον ὦ τᾶν;

ΛΑΚΩΝ

τὰν Πύλον,
ἇσπερ πάλαι δεόμεθα καὶ βλιμάττομες.

ΑΘΗΝΑΙΟΣ

μὰ τὸν Ποσειδῶ τοῦτο μέν γ᾽ οὐ δράσετε.

1165

ΛΥΣΙΣΤΡΑΤΗ

ἄφετ᾽ ὦγάθ᾽ αὐτοῖς.

ΑΘΗΝΑΙΟΣ

κᾆτα τίνα κινήσομεν;

ΛΥΣΙΣΤΡΑΤΗ

ἕτερόν γ᾽ ἀπαιτεῖτ᾽ ἀντὶ τούτου χωρίον.

ΑΘΗΝΑΙΟΣ

τὸ δεῖνα τοίνυν παράδοθ᾽ ἡμῖν τουτονὶ
πρώτιστα τὸν Ἐχινοῦντα καὶ τὸν Μηλιᾶ
κόλπον τὸν ὄπισθεν καὶ τὰ Μεγαρικὰ σκέλη.

1170

ΛΑΚΩΝ

οὐ τὼ σιὼ οὐχὶ πάντα γ᾽ ὦ λισσάνιε.

ΛΥΣΙΣΤΡΑΤΗ

ἐᾶτε, μηδὲν διαφέρου περὶ σκελοῖν.

LYSISTRATA
　　If you've done many good things for each other,
　　why go to war? Why not stop this conflict?　　　　　　[1160]
　　Why not conclude a peace? What's in the way?

*[In the negotiations which follow, the ambassadors use the body of
Reconciliation as a map of Greece, pointing to various parts to make
their points]*

SPARTAN AMBASSADOR
　　We're willing, but the part that's sticking out
　　we want that handed back.

LYSISTRATA
　　　　　　　　　　　　Which one is that?

SPARTAN AMBASSADOR *[pointing to Reconciliation's buttocks]*
　　This one here—that's Pylos. We must have that—
　　we've been aching for it a long time now.[59]

ATHENIAN AMBASSADOR
　　By Poseidon, you won't be having that!

LYSISTRATA
　　My good man, you'll surrender it to them.

ATHENIAN AMBASSADOR
　　Then how do we make trouble, stir up shit?

LYSISTRATA
　　Ask for something else of equal value.

ATHENIAN AMBASSADOR *[inspecting Reconciliation's body and pointing
　　to her public hair]*
　　Then give us this whole area in here—
　　first, there's Echinous, and the Melian Gulf,
　　the hollow part behind it, and these legs　　　　　　[1170]
　　which make up Megara.[60]

SPARTAN AMBASSADOR
　　　　　　　　　　　　By the twin gods,
　　my good man, you can't have all that!

LYSISTRATA
　　　　　　　　　　　　Let it go.
　　Don't start fighting over a pair of legs.

ΑΘΗΝΑΙΟΣ

ἤδη γεωργεῖν γυμνὸς ἀποδὺς βούλομαι.

ΛΑΚΩΝ

ἐγὼ δὲ κοπραγωγεῖν γα πρῶτα ναὶ τὼ σιώ.

ΛΥΣΙΣΤΡΑΤΗ

ἐπὴν διαλλαγῆτε, ταῦτα δράσετε.　　　　　　1175
ἀλλ' εἰ δοκεῖ δρᾶν ταῦτα, βουλεύσασθε καὶ
τοῖς ξυμμάχοις ἐλθόντες ἀνακοινώσατε.

ΑΘΗΝΑΙΟΣ

ποίοισιν ὦ τᾶν ξυμμάχοις; ἐστύκαμεν.
οὐ ταὐτὰ δόξει τοῖσι συμμάχοισι νῷν
βινεῖν ἅπασιν;　　　　　　　　　　　　　1180

ΛΑΚΩΝ

　　　　　　　τοῖσι γῶν ναὶ τὼ σιὼ
ἀμοῖσι.

ΑΘΗΝΑΙΟΣ

　　　　καὶ γὰρ ναὶ μὰ Δία Καρυστίοις.

ΛΥΣΙΣΤΡΑΤΗ

καλῶς λέγετε. νῦν οὖν ὅπως ἁγνεύσετε,
ὅπως ἂν αἱ γυναῖκες ὑμᾶς ἐν πόλει
ξενίσωμεν ὧν ἐν ταῖσι κίσταις εἴχομεν.
ὅρκους δ' ἐκεῖ καὶ πίστιν ἀλλήλοις δότε.　　1185
κἄπειτα τὴν αὑτοῦ γυναῖχ' ὑμῶν λαβὼν
ἄπεισ' ἕκαστος.

ΑΘΗΝΑΙΟΣ

　　　　　　ἀλλ' ἴωμεν ὡς τάχος.

ΛΑΚΩΝ

ἄγ' ὅπᾳ τυ λῇς.

ΑΘΗΝΑΙΟΣ

　　　　　　νὴ τὸν Δί' ὡς τάχιστ' ἄγε.

ATHENIAN AMBASSADOR
I'd like to strip and start ploughing naked.

SPARTAN AMBASSADOR
By god, yes! But me first. I'll fork manure.

LYSISTRATA
You can do those things once you've made peace.
If these terms seem good, you'll want your allies
to come here to join negotiations.

ATHENIAN AMBASSADOR
What of our allies? We've all got hard ons.
Our allies will agree this is just fine.
They're all dying to get laid!

SPARTAN AMBASSADOR
                                 Ours, as well—   [1180]
no doubt of that.

ATHENIAN AMBASSADOR
                     And the Carystians—
they'll also be on board, by Zeus.

LYSISTRATA
Well said. Now you must purify yourselves.
We women will host a dinner for you
in the Acropolis. We'll use the food
we brought here in our baskets. In there
you will make a oath and pledge your trust
in one another. Then each of you
can take his wife and go back home.

ATHENIAN AMBASSADOR
                          Let's go—
and hurry up.

SPARTAN AMBASSADOR *[to Lysistrata]*
                  Lead on. Wherever you wish.

ATHENIAN AMBASSADOR
All right by Zeus, as fast as we can go.

*[Lysistrata and Reconciliation lead the Spartan and Athenian
delegations into the Acropolis]*

ΧΟΡΟΣ

στρωμάτων δὲ ποικίλων καὶ
χλανιδίων καὶ ξυστίδων καὶ   1190
χρυσίων, ὅσ᾽ ἐστί μοι,
οὐ φθόνος ἔνεστί μοι πᾶσι παρέχειν φέρειν
τοῖς παισίν, ὁπόταν τε θυγάτηρ τινὶ κανηφορῇ.
πᾶσιν ὑμῖν λέγω λαμβάνειν τῶν ἐμῶν
χρημάτων νῦν ἔνδοθεν, καὶ   1195
μηδὲν οὕτως εὖ σεσημάν-
    θαι τὸ μὴ οὐχὶ
τοὺς ῥύπους ἀνασπάσαι,
χἄττ᾽ ⟨ἂν⟩ ἔνδον ᾖ φορεῖν.
ὄψεται δ᾽ οὐδὲν σκοπῶν, εἰ   1200
    μή τις ὑμῶν
ὀξύτερον ἐμοῦ βλέπει.

εἰ δέ τῳ μὴ σῖτος ὑμῶν
ἔστι, βόσκει δ᾽ οἰκέτας καὶ
σμικρὰ πολλὰ παιδία,   1205
ἔστι παρ᾽ ἐμοῦ λαβεῖν πυρίδια λεπτὰ μέν,
ὁ δ᾽ ἄρτος ἀπὸ χοίνικος ἰδεῖν μάλα νεανίας.
ὅστις οὖν βούλεται τῶν πενήτων ἴτω
    εἰς ἐμοῦ σάκκους ἔχων καὶ
κωρύκους, ὡς λήψεται πυ-   1210
    ρούς· ὁ Μανῆς δ᾽
οὑμὸς αὐτοῖς ἐμβαλεῖ.
πρός γε μέντοι τὴν θύραν
προαγορεύω μὴ βαδίζειν
    τὴν ἐμήν, ἀλλ᾽
εὐλαβεῖσθαι τὴν κύνα.   1215

ΑΘΗΝΑΙΟΣ Α

ἄνοιγε τὴν θύραν· παραχωρεῖν οὐ θέλεις;
ὑμεῖς τί κάθησθε; μῶν ἐγὼ τῇ λαμπάδι
ὑμᾶς κατακαύσω; φορτικὸν τὸ χωρίον.

CHORUS
    Embroidered gowns and shawls,
    robes and golden ornaments—
    everything I own—I offer you
    with an open heart. Take these things
    and let your children have them,
    if you've a daughter who will be
    a basket bearer. I tell you all
    take my possessions in my home—
    nothing is so securely closed
    you can't break open all the seals
    and take whatever's there inside.   [1200]
    But if you look, you won't see much
    unless your eyesight's really keen,
    far sharper than my own.

    If anyone is out of corn
    to feed his many tiny children
    and household slaves, at home
    I've got a few fine grains of wheat—
    a quart of those will make some bread,
    a fresh good-looking loaf. If there's a man
    who wants some bread and is in need   [1210]
    let him come with his sacks and bags
    to where I live to get his wheat.
    My servant Manes will pour it out.
    But I should tell you not to come
    too near my door—there's a dog
    you need to stay well clear of.

ATHENIAN DELEGATE A *[from inside the citadel]*
    Open the door!

[The Athenian Delegate A comes staggering out of the citadel, evidently drunk. He's carrying a torch. Other delegates in the same condition come out behind him. Athenian Delegate A bumps into someone by the door, probably one of a group of Spartan slaves standing around waiting for their masters to come out][61]

ATHENIAN DELEGATE A
                Why don't you get out of my way?
    Why are you lot sitting there? What if I
    burned you with this torch? That's a stale routine![62]

οὐκ ἂν ποιήσαιμ'. εἰ δὲ πάνυ δεῖ τοῦτο δρᾶν,
ὑμῖν χαρίσασθαι, προσταλαιπωρήσομεν.　　　　　1220

Αθηναιος Β

χἠμεῖς γε μετὰ σοῦ ξυνταλαιπωρήσομεν.
οὐκ ἄπιτε; κωκύσεσθε τὰς τρίχας μακρά.

Αθηναιος Α

οὐκ ἄπιθ', ὅπως ἂν οἱ Λάκωνες ἔνδοθεν
καθ' ἡσυχίαν ἀπίωσιν εὐωχημένοι;

Αθηναιος Β

οὔπω τοιοῦτον συμπόσιον ὄπωπ' ἐγώ.　　　　　1225
ἦ καὶ χαρίεντες ἦσαν οἱ Λακωνικοί·
ἡμεῖς δ' ἐν οἴνῳ συμπόται σοφώτατοι.

Αθηναιος Α

ὀρθῶς γ', ὅτιὴ νήφοντες οὐχ ὑγιαίνομεν·
ἢν τοὺς Ἀθηναίους ἐγὼ πείσω λέγων,
μεθύοντες ἀεὶ πανταχοῖ πρεσβεύσομεν.　　　　　1230
νῦν μὲν γὰρ ὅταν ἔλθωμεν ἐς Λακεδαίμονα
νήφοντες, εὐθὺς βλέπομεν ὅ τι ταράξομεν·
ὥσθ' ὅ τι μὲν ἂν λέγωσιν οὐκ ἀκούομεν,
ἃ δ' οὐ λέγουσι, ταῦθ' ὑπονενοήκαμεν,
ἀγγέλλομεν δ' οὐ ταὐτὰ τῶν αὐτῶν πέρι.　　　　　1235
νυνὶ δ' ἅπαντ' ἤρεσκεν· ὥστ' εἰ μέν γέ τις
ᾄδοι Τελαμῶνος, Κλειταγόρας ᾄδειν δέον,
ἐπῃνέσαμεν ἂν καὶ προσεπιωρκήσαμεν.
ἀλλ' οὑτοὶ γὰρ αὖθις ἔρχονται πάλιν
ἐς ταὐτόν. οὐκ ἐρήσετ' ὦ μαστιγίαι;　　　　　1240

138

I won't do that. Well, if I really must,
to keep you happy, I'll go through with it.   [1220]

[Athenian Delegate A chases an onlooker away with his torch]

ATHENIAN DELEGATE B *[waving a torch]*
We'll be here with you to help you do it.
Why not just leave? You may soon be screaming
for that hair of yours.

ATHENIAN DELEGATE A

                              Go on, piss off!
So the Spartans inside there can come on out
and go away in peace.

[The two Athenian delegates force the Spartan slaves away from the door]

ATHENIAN DELEGATE B
                              Well now,
I never seen a banquet quite like this.
The Spartans were delightful. As for us,
we had too much wine, but as companions
we said lots of really clever things.

ATHENIAN DELEGATE A
That's right. When we're sober, we lose our minds.
I'll speak up and persuade Athenians
what when our embassies go anywhere   [1230]
they stay permanently drunk. As it is,
whenever we go sober off to Sparta,
right away we look to stir up trouble.
So we just don't hear what they have to say
and get suspicious of what they don't state.
Then we bring back quite different reports
about the same events. But now these things
have all been sorted out. So if someone there
sang "Telamon" when he should have sung
"Cleitagora," we'd applaud the man
and even swear quite falsely that . . .[63]

[The Spartan slaves they forced away from the door are gradually coming back]

                              Hey, those slaves
are coming here again. You whipping posts,   [1240]
why can't you go away?

139

ΑΘΗΝΑΙΟΣ Β
  νὴ τὸν Δί᾽ ὡς ἤδη γε χωροῦσ᾽ ἔνδοθεν.

ΛΑΚΩΝ
  ὦ Πολυχαρείδα λαβὲ τὰ φυσατήρια,
  ἵν᾽ ἐγὼ διποδιάξω τε κἀείσω καλὸν
  ἐς τὼς Ἀσαναίως τε καὶ ἐς ἡμᾶς ἅμα.

ΑΘΗΝΑΙΟΣ
  λαβὲ δῆτα τὰς φυσαλλίδας πρὸς τῶν θεῶν,   1245
  ὡς ἥδομαί γ᾽ ὑμᾶς ὁρῶν ὀρχουμένους.

ΛΑΚΩΝ
          ὅρμαον
      τὼς κυρσανίως ὦ Μναμοῦνα
        τάν τ᾽ ἐμὰν Μῶαν, ἅτις
      οἶδεν ἀμὲ τώς τ᾽ Ἀσαναίως,   1250
        ὅκα τοὶ μὲν ἐπ᾽ Ἀρταμιτίῳ
        πρώκροον σιοείκελοι
      ποττὰ κᾶλα τὼς Μήδως τ᾽ ἐνίκων,
        ἀμὲ δ᾽ αὖ Λεωνίδας
        ἆγεν περ τὼς κάπρως   1255
      θάγοντας οἰῶ τὸν ὀδόντα·
  πολὺς δ᾽ ἀμφὶ τὰς γένυας ἀφρὸς ἤνσει,
  πολὺς δ᾽ ἁμᾷ καττῶν σκελῶν ἀφρὸς ἵετο.
        ἦν γὰρ τὤνδρες οὐκ ἐλάσσως   1260
        τᾶς ψάμμας τοὶ Πέρσαι.
      ἀγροτέρα σηροκτόνε
      μόλε δεῦρο παρσένε σιὰ
        ποττὰς σπονδάς,
  ὡς συνέχῃς πολὺν ἀμὲ χρόνον.   1265
  νῦν δ᾽ αὖ φιλία τ᾽ αἰὲς εὔπορος εἴη
        ταῖς συνθήκαις,
  καὶ τᾶν αἱμυλᾶν ἀλωπέκων παυσαίμεθα.
      ὦ δεῦρ᾽ ἴθι δεῦρ᾽ ὦ
        κυναγὲ παρσένε.   1270

ATHENIAN DELEGATE B
By Zeus,
the ones in there are coming out again.

[The Spartan delegates come out of the citadel. The Spartan ambassador is carrying a musical instrument]

SPARTAN AMBASSADOR
Here, my dear sir, take this wind instrument,
so I can dance and sing a lovely song
to honour both Athenians and ourselves.

ATHENIAN AMBASSADOR *[turning to one of the slaves]*
Yes, by the gods, take the pipes. I love
to see you Spartans dance and sing.

[The music starts. The Spartan Ambassador sings and dances]

SPARTAN AMBASSADOR
O Memory, to this young man
send down your child the Muse
who knows the Spartans and Athenians.[64]   [1250]
Back then at Artemesium
they fought the ships like gods of war
and overpowered the Medes,
while we, I know, led by Leonidas
whetted our teeth like boars
with foaming mouths, which dripped
down on our legs. The Persian force
possessed more fighting men
than grains of sea shore sand.   [1260]
O Artemis, queen of the wild,
slayer of beasts, chaste goddess,
come here to bless our treaty,
to make us long united.
May our peace be always blessed
with friendship and prosperity,
and may we put an end
to all manipulating foxes.   [1270]
Come here, O come here,
Virgin Goddess of the Hunt.

[Lysistrata emerges from the citadel bringing all the wives with her]

Aristophanes

ΛΥΣΙΣΤΡΑΤΗ

ἄγε νυν ἐπειδὴ τἄλλα πεποίηται καλῶς,
ἀπάγεσθε ταύτας ὦ Λάκωνες, τάσδε τε
ὑμεῖς· ἀνὴρ δὲ παρὰ γυναῖκα καὶ γυνὴ   1275
στήτω παρ' ἄνδρα, κᾆτ' ἐπ' ἀγαθαῖς συμφοραῖς
ὀρχησάμενοι θεοῖσιν εὐλαβώμεθα
τὸ λοιπὸν αὖθις μὴ 'ξαμαρτάνειν ἔτι.

ΧΟΡΟΣ

πρόσαγε χορόν, ἔπαγε <δὲ> Χάριτας,
        ἐπὶ δὲ κάλεσον Ἄρτεμιν,   1280
        ἐπὶ δὲ δίδυμον ἀγέχορον
            Ἰήιον
    εὔφρον', ἐπὶ δὲ Νύσιον,
ὃς μετὰ μαινάσι Βάκχιος ὄμμασι δαίεται,
        Δία τε πυρὶ φλεγόμενον, ἐπί τε   1285
        πότνιαν ἄλοχον ὀλβίαν·
    εἶτα δὲ δαίμονας, οἷς ἐπιμάρτυσι
    χρησόμεθ' οὐκ ἐπιλήσμοσιν
    Ἡσυχίας πέρι τῆς ἀγανόφρονος,
        ἣν ἐποίησε θεὰ Κύπρις.   1290
        ἀλαλαὶ ἰὴ παιήων·
            αἴρεσθ' ἄνω ἰαί,
        ὡς ἐπὶ νίκῃ ἰαί.
    εὐοῖ εὐοῖ, εὐαί εὐαί.

ΛΥΣΙΣΤΡΑΤΗ

πρόφαινε δὴ σὺ Μοῦσαν ἐπὶ νέᾳ νέαν.   1295

ΛΑΚΩΝ

    Ταΰγετον αὖτ' ἐραννὸν ἐκλιπῶα
    Μῶα μόλε Λάκαινα πρεπτὸν ἁμὶν
        κλέωα τὸν Ἀμύκλαις σιὸν
        καὶ χαλκίοικον Ἀσάναν,   1300
        Τυνδαρίδας τ' ἀγασώς,

142

LYSISTRATA65

Come now, since everything has turned out well,
take these women back with you, you Spartans.
And, you Athenians, these ones are yours.
Let each man stand beside his wife, each wife
beside her man, and then to celebrate
good times let's dance in honour of the gods.
And for all future time, let's never make
the same mistake again.

[The Chorus now sings to the assembled group, as the wives and husbands are rejoined]

CHORUS

Lead on the dance, bring on the Graces,
and summon Artemis and her twin,   [1280]
Apollo, the god who heals us all,
call on Bacchus, Nysa's god,
whose eyes blaze forth
amid his Maenads' ecstasy,
and Zeus alight with flaming fire,
and Hera, Zeus' blessed wife,
and other gods whom we will use
as witnesses who won't forget
the meaning of the gentle Peace
made her by goddess Aphrodite.   [1290]

Alalai! Raise the cry of joy,
raise it high, iai!
the cry of victory, iai!
Evoi, evoi, evoi, evoi!

LYSISTRATA

Spartan, now offer us another song,
match our new song with something new.

SPARTAN AMBASSADOR

Leave lovely Taygetus once again
and, Spartan Muse, in some way
that is appropriate for us
pay tribute to Amyclae's god,
and to bronze-housed Athena,
to Tyndareus' splendid sons,   [1300]

τοὶ δὴ πὰρ Εὐρώταν ψιάδδοντι.
  εἷα μάλ᾽ ἔμβη
  ὢ εἷα κοῦφα πάλλων,
  ὡς Σπάρταν ὑμνίωμες,   1305
  τᾷ σιῶν χοροὶ μέλοντι
    καὶ ποδῶν κτύπος,
  ᾇ τε πῶλοι ταὶ κόραι
  πὰρ τὸν Εὐρωταν
  ἀμπάλλοντι πυκνὰ ποδοῖν   1310
    ἀγκονίωαι,
ταὶ δὲ κόμαι σείονθ᾽ περ Βακχᾶν
  θυρσαδδωᾶν καὶ παιδδωᾶν.
  ἀγεῖται δ᾽ ἁ Λήδας παῖς
  ἁγνὰ χοραγὸς εὐπρεπής.   1315
ἀλλ᾽ ἄγε κόμαν παραμπύκιδδε χερί, ποδοῖν τε πάδη
ᾇ τις ἔλαφος· κρότον δ᾽ ἁμᾷ ποίει χορωφελήταν.
καὶ τὰν σιὰν δ᾽ αὖ τὰν κρατίσταν Χαλκίοικον ὕμνει 1320
  τὰν πάμμαχον.

who play beside the Eurotas.
Step now, with many a nimble turn,
so we may sing a hymn to Sparta,
dancing in honour of the gods,
with stamping feet in that place
where by the river Eurotas
young maidens dance,
like fillies raising dust,   [1310]
tossing their manes,
like bacchants who play
and wave their thyrsus stalks,
brought on by Leda's lovely child,
their holy leader in the choral dance.[66]

But come let your hands bind up your hair.
Let your feet leap up like deer, sound out the beat
to help our dance. Sing out a song of praise
for our most powerful bronze-house goddess,
all-conquering Athena!

[They all exit singing and dancing]

NOTES

1   Lysistrata is complaining that if the city had called a major festival all the women would be in the streets enjoying themselves. But none of them, it seems, has answered her invitation to a meeting (as we find out a few lines further on).

2   At the time *Lysistrata* was first produced, the Athenians and Spartans had been fighting for many years. The Boeotians were allies of the Spartans. Boeotia was famous for its eels, considered a luxury item in Athens.

3   The two goddesses are Demeter and her daughter Persephone. The Athenian women frequently invoke them.

4   Theogenes was a well-known merchant and ship owner.

5   Calonice is making an obscure joke on the name Anagyrus, a political district named after a bad-smelling plant.

6   In Aristophanes' text, Lampito and other Spartans use a parody of a Spartan dialect, a style of speaking significantly different from (although related to) Athenian Greek. Translators have dealt with this in different ways, usually by giving the Spartans a recognizable English dialect, for example, from the Southern States or Scotland, or English with a foreign accent. The difference between the Spartans' speech and the language of the others reflects the political antagonism between the Athenians and Spartans. Here I have not tried to follow this trend. My main reasons for doing so are (in brief) that, first, some dialects are in places incomprehensible to some readers or have been made irrelevant (e.g., Jack Lindsay's Scottish language in the Bantam edition of Aristophanes or the erratic Russian English of the Perseus translation) and, second, I wish to leave the choice of dialect or accent up to the imagination of the readers or the directors of stage productions (who might like to experiment with dialects which will connect with their particular audiences more immediately than any one I might select).

7   Spartans commonly invoke the divine twins Castor and Pollux, brothers of Helen and Clytaemnestra.

8   Thrace is a region to the north of Greece, a long way from Athens. Eucrates was an Athenian commander in the region. Pylos is a small

area in the south Peloponnese which the Athenians had occupied for a number of years.

9   Miletus had rebelled against Athens in the previous year. That city was associated with sexuality and (in this case) the manufacture of sexual toys.

10   Taygetus was a high mountain in the Peloponnese.

11   In a famous story, Menelaus went storming through Troy looking for his wife, Helen, in order to kill her. But when he found her, he was so overcome by her beauty that he relented and took her back home to Sparta.

12   Pherecrates was an Athenian comic dramatist. The line may be a quotation from one of his plays.

13   The financial reserves of the Athenian state were stored in the Acropolis

14   Lycon's wife was an Athenian famous for her promiscuity.

15   Cleomenes, a king of Sparta, once came with a small army to Athens (in 508) to help the oligarch party. He had a very hostile reception and took refuge in the Acropolis, where he stayed under siege for two days. A truce was arranged and the Spartans left peacefully.

16   Euripides is the famous tragic dramatist, a younger contemporary of Aristophanes. Marathon was the site of the great Greek victory of the Persian expeditionary forces in 490 BC, a high point of Athenian military achievement.

17   The reference to Lemnian fire is not clear. The island of Lemnos perhaps had some volcanic activity, or else the reference is to the women of Lemnos who killed all their husbands. There is a pun on the Greek word for *Lemnos* and the word in the same speech referring to material in the eye.

18   Samos is an important island near Athens. A number of the generals of Athenian forces came from there.

19   Sommerstein observes (p. 171) that the epithet Tritogeneia ("Trito born") refers to Athena's birth beside the River Triton or Lake Tritonis in North Africa.

20   Boupalus was a sculptor from Chios.

21 The Achelous was a large well-known river in northern Greece.

22 Sabazius was a popular foreign god associated with drinking (like Diony-sus). Adonis was a mortal youth loved by Aphrodite. An annual festival was celebrated in his memory. Demostrates was a politician promoting the disastrous Athenian military expedition to Sicily. Zacynthus is an island off the Peloponnese, an ally of Athens.

23 OLD WOMAN A: In modern productions the old women who speak in this scene either come out of the gates to the Acropolis or are members of the Chorus. Alternatively the speeches could be assigned to the characters we have met earlier (Myrrhine and Calonice), who have emerged from the Acropolis behind Lysistrata.

24 Black eyes were treated with a small cup placed over the eye to reduce the swelling.

25 The armed guards accompanying the Magistrate are traditionally Scythian archers.

26 Cranaus was a legendary king of Athens.

27 Peisander was a leading Athenian politician, suspected of favouring the war for selfish reasons.

28 Corybantes were divine attendants on the foreign goddess Cybele. They were associated with ecstatic music and dancing.

29 Shields with monstrous Gorgon's heads depicted on them were common in Athens.

30 Tereus was a mythical king of Thrace and a popular figure with Athenian dramatists.

31 A honey cake was traditionally part of the funeral service. It was given to make sure the dead shade reached Hades.

32 Charon is the ferryman who transports the shades of the dead across the river into Hades.

33 Hippias was a tyrant in Athens from 528 to 510. Cleisthenes, an Athenian, was a favourite target of Aristophanes, ridiculed as a passive homosexual. Here there's an accusation that he is sympathetic to the Spartans. The pay the old men refer to is a daily payment of three obols from the state to jury men.

34 Aritogeiton and his friend Harmodius assassinated the tyrant Hipparchus, the brother of Hippias. The two were celebrated as heroes of democratic Athens.

35 The Old Women are referring to many city activities and rituals in which girls of noble families played important roles. The phrase "pounding barley" refers to making cakes for sacrifices.

36 Leipsydrion was the site of a battle years before when the tyrant Hippias besieged and defeated his opponents. The old men are treating the event as if they had been victorious. The detail about their white feet, Sommerstein suggests, refers to those who were hostile to Hippias and the tyrants (hence, lovers of freedom).

37 Artemesia was queen of Halicarnassus in Asia Minor. She led ships from her city as part of the Persian expedition against Athens in 480 and fought at the Battle of Salamis.

38 Micon was a well-known Athenian painter.

39 This is a reference to an old story in which the dung beetle got its revenge against an eagle by smashing its eggs. The old woman obviously threatens the man's testicles as she says this.

40 Hecate was a goddess whose worship was associated with, among other things, birth and children.

41 Orsilochus is either a well known seducer or someone who keeps a brothel.

42 To have a child in a holy place, like the Acropolis, was considered a sacrilege.

43 Myronides and Phormio were two dead generals who fought for Athens.

44 Sommerstein (p. 200) points out that Paeonidae is a political district in northern Attica. The name suggest the Greek verb *paiein*, meaning to *strike* or *copulate*. Sommerstein offers the translation "Bangwell." Jack Lindsay translates the place as "Bangtown."

45 Hercules was famous for always being hungry and having an enormous appetite.

46 Cynalopex (meaning "Fox Dog") was the nickname of Philostratus who apparently was a pimp.

47   Prytanes was the business committee of the Athenian council.

48   The Greek reads "we need Pellene," an area in the Peloponnese allied with Sparta. But, as Sommerstein points out (p. 206), this is undoubtedly a pun invoking a word meaning *vagina* or *anus*. In the exchanges which follow, the Spartans are depicted as having a decided preference for anal sex.

49   Pan was a god associated with wild unrestrained sex in the wilderness.

50   The meaning of the Greek word *hussakos* (here translated as *honey pots*) is very obscure. Sommerstein translates as "pork barrels."

51   Lamplighters had to walk along bent over in order to protect the flame they carried.

52   Tricorynthus is a region in Attica, near Marathon. Presumably it was famous for its insects.

53   Carystus is a state from Euboea, allied to Athens.

54   Cleisthenes was a well known Athenian, whom Aristophanes frequently ridicules as a passive homosexual.

55   In 415 the statues of Hermes in Athens were mutilated by having their penises chopped off, a very sacrilegious act .

56   In Aristophanes' time, this character (Reconciliation) would be played by a man with a body stocking prominently displaying female characteristics: breasts, pubic hair, buttocks.

57   Lysistrata is listing some of the festivals where all the Greek states cooperated in the ritual celebrations.

58   In 464 Sparta suffered a massive earthquake, which killed many citizens. Their slaves, who included the Messenians, rose in revolt. Sparta appealed to Athens for help, and the Athenians, after some debate, sent Cimon with an army to assist the Spartans.

59   Pylos was a small but important part of the south Peloponnese which the Athenians had seized in 425 and held onto ever since.

60   Echinous, Melian Gulf, and Megara are places relatively close to Athens.

61   The stage business at this point is somewhat confusing. It's not clear whether the Athenian delegates who now appear are leaving the meeting in the citadel or arriving and wanting to get in. Here I follow

Sommerstein, who is following Henderson, and have the delegates emerge from the meeting. The people hanging around the door are probably the slaves who came with the Spartans and who are waiting for their masters inside.

62 This comment is taking a swipe at other comic dramatists who use a stock set of situations or actions, while at the same time the action uses the stock technique (not an uncommon feature of Aristophanic comedy).

63 "Telamon" and "Cleitagora" are well known drinking songs.

64 The Spartan Ambassador is singing about two famous battles against the Persians (both in 480), the Athenian naval victory at Artemisium and the Spartan stand of the 300 at Thermopylae. This military campaign was an important highlight of Greek unity.

65 There is some dispute about who this speech should be assigned to. Sommerstein (p. 221) has a useful summary of the arguments.

66 Taygetus is an important mountain in Sparta. Amyclae's god is Apollo who had a shrine at Amyclae, near Sparta. Bronze-housed Athena is a reference to the shrine of Athena in Sparta. Tyndareus' splendid sons are Castor and Pollux, the twin gods (brothers of Helen and Cly-taemnestra). The Eurotas is a river near Sparta. The thyrsus stalk is a plant stem held by the followers of Bacchus in their ecstatic dancing. Leda's child is Helen (wife of Menelaus, sister of Castor and Pollux and Clytaemnestra, a child of Zeus).

CPSIA information can be obtained
at www.ICGtesting.com
Printed in the USA
FSHW010951071221
86750FS